POWER
AND
AUTHORITY
IN LAW
ENFORCEMENT

POWER
AND
AUTHORITY
IN LAW
ENFORCEMENT

Edited by

TERRY R. ARMSTRONG, Ph.D.

Fellow in Social Science
Park College-Crown Center
Kansas City, Missouri

KENNETH M. CINNAMON, Ph.D.

Gestalt and Social Competency Institute
Shawnee Mission, Kansas

With a Foreword by

Donald Kreps, Ph.D.,

Chairman, Department of Sociology
Park College, Kansas City, Missouri

CHARLES C THOMAS • PUBLISHER
Springfield • Illinois • U.S.A.

Published and Distributed Throughout the World by

CHARLES C THOMAS ● PUBLISHER

Bannerstone House

301-327 East Lawrence Avenue, Springfield, Illinois, U.S.A.

© *1976, by* CHARLES C THOMAS ● PUBLISHER

ISBN 0-398-03571-7

Library of Congress Catalog Card Number: 76-7384

Printed in the United States of America

R-1

Library of Congress Cataloging in Publication Data

Main entry under title:
Power and authority in law enforcement,
    CONTENTS: Introduction. --Theoretical perspec-
tives: Armstrong, T. R. The roots of power.
Fairfield, R. The paradox of power. Crozier, M.
The problem of power. De George, R. T. The concept of authority. Whisenand, P. and Ferguson, F.
Controlling: the use of authority, power, and
intelligence. --Applied perspectives: Becker, H. K.
Historical-philosophical development of administra-
tion. [etc.]
    1. Police--Addresses, essays, lectures.
    2. Power (Social sciences)--Addresses, essays,
lectures.   3. Authority-Addresses, essays,
lectures.   4. Law enforcement-Addresses, essays
lectures. I. Armstrong, Terry R., 1946-
II. Cinnamon, Kenneth M.
HV7921.P67   1976   363.2   76-7384
ISBN 0-398-03571-7

CONTRIBUTORS

Terry R. Armstrong, Ph.D., is a Fellow in Social Science at Park College-Crown Center in Kansas City, Missouri.

Harold K. Becker, D.Crim., is Director of the Center for Criminal Justice at California State University in Long Beach.

Kenneth M. Cinnamon, Ph.D., is a staff psychologist at the Wyandot Mental Health Center and an associate of the Gestalt and Social Competency Institute in Shawnee Mission, Kansas.

Michel Crozier is an internationally known sociologist who is read widely in the United States.

Richard T. De George, Ph.D., is Professor of Philosophy at the University of Kansas.

Roy P. Fairfield, Ph.D., is Professor of Social Science at Union Graduate School and Antioch College.

R. Fred Ferguson, M.S., is the Chief of Police in Riverside, California.

Bernard Lubin, Ph.D., is Professor of Psychology at the University of Missouri at Kansas City.

Philip A. Mann, Ph.D., is Associate Professor of Psychology at Indiana University, Bloomington, Indiana.

Franklin W. Neff, Ed.D., is Program Director of Evaluation Studies at the Institute for Community Studies, University of Missouri at Kansas City.

Paul M. Whisenand, Ph.D., is Chairman, Department of Criminology, at California State University, Long Beach.

dedicated to Anne Armstrong
Jerry and Susan Freedman and
Shelley — with our love

FOREWORD

THE use and abuse of power has always been of concern to those who study the many problems of social life. The desire to understand the sources of power, and the motivations of those who exercise power is, therefore, no new phenomenon. But until recently, these matters were almost exclusively confined to the speculations of philosophers or to the machinations of political leaders. Then the sciences of human behavior began to develop, and the study of power as a universal phenomenon was undertaken. The ensuing decades, particularly from the latter half of the 19th century to the present, have produced a number of analyses and theoretical statements on the sources and uses of power.

Not until the 1960s did social power become a major concern of social science researchers and theorists; and even so, our knowledge of this phenomenon is woefully inadequate. This anthology first provides some theoretical perspectives on the problems of power and authority, and then illustrates the actual uses of power and authority in and by police organizations. Society, of course, gives the police organizations the authority (the legitimate right to use power) to uphold and enforce the law. It is not unusual to observe, however, that the police often exceed the limits of their authority by utilizing power beyond that conferred on them by society. The writers in the second section of this volume attempt to illustrate this phenomenon by examining both internal aspects of police organization and the operations of the police in their relationships with the community.

The presentations of both theoretical and applied aspects of power, with its focus on police organization, should make this volume useful, either as a text or as an adjunct to other basic texts for a number of courses in the criminal justice, sociology, and political science curricula.

Donald Kreps, Ph.D.

ix

INTRODUCTION

ALTHOUGH the study of power began with the earliest philosophers, the phenomenon of power has become more complex and threatening to human survival. The concept of power is no longer only an academic consideration that social scientists and philosophers use as a tool for understanding the *whys* of political and social behavior. Man's future now depends on *how* accumulated instruments of power will be used in the practical affairs of world politics, law enforcement, and the administration of justice.

An understanding of power is of special significance for the law enforcement official. Because our future may well be contingent upon the uses of police power, it is imperative that we seriously reflect upon this human phenomena. If we are to create a just world we must be extremely careful about the alternatives we select — we must understand what we are doing and why.

For many, power has become a *taboo* with which they do not want to be associated. In light of contemporary experience this reaction is understandable. Therefore, if we are to run and hide our heads in the proverbial sand we may be destroyed without having the foresight to avert disaster. The possible destruction of the world by atomic holocaust would be an extreme case of the abuse of power. No less appealing are the many possibilities of abuse within our policing system.

It is not our purpose to frighten the reader into thinking about power and authority as they relate to the administration of justice — that would cause the very opposite of what we hope to accomplish with this anthology. Many already react emotionally toward police power instead of attempting to understand and respect the power while finding ways to limit possible abuses of it. For those concerned about power and authority in law enforcement, this short collection is but an introduction and source book, and does not cover the subject completely. The first half of the book deals with perceptions and conceptualizations of power and authority — even at the risk of being considered too theoretical. For we believe that all too often the theoretical framework for the applied usage of power has been set aside with unfortunate consequences.

After viewing various definitions of power we have attempted to focus on the human factor — what the wielding of power and authority does to the individuals involved — and on the concerns and dilemmas of law enforcement officers who must sometimes use others as means to presumably greater ends. The interdependence of power and moral concern traditionally belongs to the study of ethics and, more recently, to social psychology; but whatever we may wish to call the study of this area of human concern, it remains a necessary field of analysis for all concerned with the administration of justice.

Power is institutional as well as personal, and in the twentieth century it seems as if the *real power* is within the large police and military organizations. Indeed, it is impossible to understand power without looking at these institutional structures and how they wield influence over society and individuals. In the last few years police power has increased to previously unthinkable proportions and its abuses are continually reported by the media. It is a kind of power that concerns present day social scientists considerably, but it is only a single aspect of power — to look solely at it would bias our understanding and only add to an already confused situation.

Police power has many faces. At one moment it protects the status quo and at another it is the vehicle of social change. It is reflected by authority, in legitimacy and unionism, and in external political processes. Because of its ever-changing characteristics it is difficult to comprehend; yet intuitively, out of our living processes, we all understand, at least in a crude way, what police power is. Our individual definitions of police power vary according to the ways we have personally encountered it and how we have used it or been controlled by it.

No matter our means of livelihood or intellectual bent, an understanding of power and authority in the administration of justice is imperative. Whether we like it or not, *policing* means to have power over and at the same time to be powerless.

With the abuses of police power that recent events and committee investigations have brought to our attention, teachers, students, and others have found it necessary to question the very structure of our law enforcement establishment. No doubt more books and articles will be written in the coming decade about these power relationships than were written in any previous decade in American history. Citizens will have to read them carefully, but most important, they will need some conceptual understanding of power, authority, and human values in order to think critically about the ways in which we might modify our law enforcement system and the administration of justice processes. It is tempting to bring a collection of essays together that will focus primarily on the negative aspects of power — especially police power. We have been exceedingly careful to avoid this. It is more important to develop a critical attitude than to resort to emotional reactions. This critical attitude is important to the development of a theoretical framework corroborated by experience, so that each of us might begin our own critical appraisal of power in the administration of justice.

It is often easier simply to observe others using and abusing power rather than to analyze the process. We each possess power over one another. Each of us makes power decisions everyday, often without realizing that we are affecting the lives of other human beings. Every human act is guided by our personal sense of morality, regardless of how distorted it may be.

Power, authority, and the administration of justice are the primary focal points of this anthology. It is difficult to look at these power relationships objectively; therefore, we have attempted to widen the scope of understanding concerning their complexities.

The objective of this anthology is not to provide a thorough account of power but to analyze some of its ramifications in the law enforcement establishment and in the administration of justice. Those in and outside the law enforcement establishment, as well as students in the social sciences, will be able to use this anthology as a springboard into research and critical thinking. It is to be hoped this collection will help the reader become sensitive to the critical relationships between power and authority and the administration of justice, as well as generate new ideas about these unexplored phenomena.

CONTENTS

POWER
AND
AUTHORITY
IN LAW
ENFORCEMENT

Theoretical Perspectives

THE theoretical implications of power and authority are diverse and complex. The concept of power is often elusive because it accompanies all social processes; like many aspects of collective life it is easier to ignore than to understand. Pointedly, Michel Crozier states the problem: "The taboo about power is still perhaps more profoundly rooted in the conscience of modern man than the taboo about sex."

Many individuals attempt to minimize the reality of power. Possessing power and/or authority often is treated as if it were as humiliating as some of our less respectable social diseases. Paradoxically, a significant number of texts dealing with law enforcement leave the phenomena of power and its implications unattended.

In this section, Armstrong, Fairfield, Crozier, De George, Whisenand, and Ferguson explore the roots of power and authority. Among the many crucial questions addressed are:

What is power?

What is authority?

How does power affect our behavior?

What is the psychology of power?

What are the dangers of power and authority?

Who possesses power and authority?

How do we achieve power and authority?

Within what systems does power exist?

How do we lose power and authority?

How may we use power and authority most effectively?

We urge readers to carefully consider the issues raised in this section and to apply them to their past, present, and future endeavors. Our society has awakened to the stark realization that abuses of power and authority can easily become the norm rather than the exception. It is our hope that by presenting the primary issues surrounding power and authority readers will be better

equipped to critically assess their personal and working environ-
ments. We hope the following articles will serve as a springboard,
or even a catalyst, in helping to pave the way for more responsible
and responsive behavior.

THE ROOTS OF POWER

TERRY R. ARMSTRONG

POWER — some men have it without wanting it and others want it without having it. Some men are power seekers, searching out power relationships in order to use them for their own ends while others abdicate their power because they value something or someone else above power.[1]

There is a difference between the power circumstances and philosophies that motivate men towards or away from the pinnacles of power. On one hand are the institutions, geographies, technologies, and populations which make the concentrations of power possible, and on the other are the philosophies, values, and fantasies which give direction to men's actions.

It is impossible to understand the power process without investigating these two facets and their interactions within the boundaries of existing social conditions or environment.

It is less difficult to describe objectively and analyze the instruments of power — like nature, they are nonmoral — than it is to evaluate the motives of the men controlling it. The values held by the men in the critical positions of authority were not instilled by gods or demons, but by the society and social conditions from which they sprung.

Thus, a power system exists which consists of three major interacting elements: (1) nonmoral technologies, (2) individual motives and values, and (3) the social conditions and cultural heritage, including institutions.

Whenever we try to analyze man and his social actions we find we cannot follow strict rules of logic. The reason for this is that human relationships are dynamic, and any static model we abstract from our observations of social man are not *real* but only useful conceptualizations.

When nonmoral technology is separated from value-laden man, two conceptual categories are being constructed for the sake of analysis. The premise developed is that all *A* is not *B* and all *B* is not *A*, and a known fact is that there is some *AB*. In other words, values do play a role in the development of technologies. The very science that brought about the technological revolution was motivated by value. Men cannot escape values and science cannot escape men.

Thus, for this analysis of power, I will call technologies nonmoral, knowing full well that I may some day write an essay or treatise on the moral aspects of technology.

> In short, the concepts of influence and power are extremely general, and have reference to a wide range of interpersonal relations. This analysis can be carried to whatever level of refinement is required by the particular problem at hand. But political phenomena are only obscured by the pseudosimplification attained with any unitary conception of power as being always and everywhere the same (violence or economic power...). What is common to all power and influence relations is only effect on policy. What is affected and on what basis are variables whose specific content in a given situation can be determined only by inquiry into the actual practices of the actors in that situation.[2]

As Lasswell and others have pointed out, power is ever changing — forever finding new ways to express itself. This is true because power is of men; it is of their making. Indeed if we are to find the roots of power we must search for the roots of man.

People must first survive the elements of nature, and then must survive the attacks of other people, and the results of their own doing. People are not the only creatures who possess powers. Even the very elements have power to move themselves from place to place. We call this power, energy. People, by harnessing the forces of energy for their own ends, have gained power. The source of this power was not the crude elements themselves but man's capacity for abstraction. Through abstraction man "has transformed the planet, annihilated space, and trebled the world's population."[3]

The rational ordering of the elements made it possible for man to use them to his advantage, just as the turning of economics into a rational semipredictable system gave some men even more power than others. The complex technologies and exorbitant institutions that mold our lives are the concrete power tools generated by people's ability to rationalize and systematize.

Through abstraction people forged social institutions which provided enlightenment as well as servitude, and when they combined abstraction with experimentation, they developed a science that would free them from the fears of starvation while providing them with the fear of human extinction. Through abstraction they created the image of hell but by experimentation they created hell.

We obviously know if one group or individual is more powerful than another, and crude estimates can be arrived at; but, as yet we cannot measure power. A power calculus has not been developed because of methodological weaknesses — we cannot even define the concept. "Many have exchanged the terms 'power,' 'influence,' 'control,' 'authority,' 'leadership,' for each other at will and in so doing have added considerably to the confusion."[4] However, it would be dangerous to state categorically that a political mathematics cannot be developed. Not surprisingly, some economists have already adapted some simple models and their efforts will no doubt reap results.[5]

The aspect of power which interests me the most is the *desire for power*.

> Various desires have dominated the work of philosophers. There is the desire to know, and what is by no means the same thing, the desire to prove that the world is knowable. There is the desire for happiness, the desire for virtue, and — a synthesis of these two — the desire for salvation. There is the desire for the sense of union with God or with other human beings. There is the desire for beauty, the desire for enjoyment, and, finally the desire for power.[6]

Too often when any one desire dominates a person's wishes he becomes a wretched human being. When an individual in a position of power is motivated by the love of power, a Hitler is created; and when a man is filled with the love of power and denied the instruments of power he will most probably be torn to pieces as Nietzsche was. When a philosophy or ethics of power is contrived, any sense of social responsibility is rejected in favor of the heroic ruler.

> Men who allow their love of power to give them a distorted
> view of the world are to be found in every asylum: one man will
> think he is the Governor of the Bank of England, another will
> think he is the King, and yet another will think he is God.
> Highly similar delusions, if expressed by educated men in ob-
> scure language, lead to professorships of philosophy; and if
> expressed by emotional men in eloquent language, lead to dic-
> tatorships. *Certified* lunatics are shut up because of their prone-
> ness to violence when their pretensions are questioned; the
> *uncertified* variety are given the control of powerful armies, and
> can inflict death and disaster upon all sane men within their
> reach. The success of insanity in literature, in philosophy, and
> in politics, is one of the peculiarities of our age. And the suc-
> cessful form of insanity proceeds almost entirely from impulses
> toward power.[7]

Russell's monsters are propagated when the desire for power
becomes the dominant motivating force. In most cases the will to
power collides with other desires and external powers so that the
new-born child discovers his powers through the struggle of existence. At first his only power is that of existence; he demands from
his mother's system the ingredients of life and growth. After his
birth the ability to cry is the only power he has over his environment. This power is essentially the ability to manipulate through
oral communication. As the child grows he develops a complex
language system and learns to crawl, walk and run. The child
explores himself and his environment, discovering himself and
others. He tests his potentials against others and the environment,
and experiences ecstasy when he succeeds, and anxiety when he
does not meet his own expectations. As he matures into puberty
the body craves new excitements because of potential sexual inter-
course. This new power creates anxiety because of new relationships and new responsibilities.[8]

As humans strive to fulfill their own potential they are faced
with the desires of other humans and with mammoth systems of
beliefs and ethics, many of which contradict their will to become.
This creates a struggle between the individual and the culture
which demands obedience to its rather rigid standards of behavior.

The struggle between the individual and his culture breeds conflict. In some instances, a creative conflict emerges from the dialectical process. In others, aggression and violence erupt. In order for power to concentrate, the will of individuals must be subordinated to the group, institution, state, etc. The concept of the Social Contract as proclaimed by Locke, Hume, and Rousseau is not far off here.

Institutions and states augment their potency by building upon the accumulations of knowledge derived from the creative conflict emerging from the dialectical struggle between the individual and his environment. The successful institution must simultaneously control violence so that the creative process is not totally occupied with devising means to check human aggression.

> All forms of political organization have a bias in favor of the exploitation of some kinds of conflict and the suppression of others because *organization is the mobilization of bias*. Some isssues are organized into politics while others are organized out.[9]

Political organization resides within a communal structure that has long been identified as the state. It is through the state and its subinstitutions that power is exercised. The source of power is man's ability to abstract; through abstraction he has created and accumulated technology and sociotechnological systems. It is through these institutions that power is exerted. But institutions exist in societies, not in vacuums. They are established to meet group needs, which in turn serve to legalize the exercise of power through granted authority.

The state "is a human creation invented by certain men and upheld by certain virtues and fundamental qualities which the men of yesterday had and which may vanish into air tomorrow."[10] The ordinary man sees within the state and other massive institutions an "anonymous power"[11] whose origins he cannot fathom. He lives within their spheres of influence and eludes their dynamism with the cunning of a Cro-Magnon man evading the dangers of the wild. The everyday citizen respects these institutions out of fear. He lives beneath their shadow and comfort. Though the average citizen has not created these institutions, their continuing existence depends upon the *general will*, or what is now known as public opinion. A whole branch of Political Science is dedicated to the study of this concept initiated by Machiavelli, expanded by Rousseau, and defined by nearly everybody.

Public opinion vacillates, and so it has been necessary to create laws. Laws are but written documents which dictate what men shall and shall not do. They are not the primary source of man's power but have become tools of power because of the threat of punishment they convey.

The laws of a society do not create power but channel it. Laws explain how the institutions of a society are constructed and how control of institutional power is decided. They provide for orderly transfer of power and wealth. In some societies, custom or religion serve in the place of written secular law.

De Tocqueville observed,

> ... the less coercive and dictatorial the political institutions of a society became, the more it needed a system of sacred belief to help restrain the actions of both the rulers and the ruled.[12]

What De Tocqueville noticed, Berle generalized into a law. "Power invariably fills any vacuum in human organization."[13] Because peace and order are necessary for a society to exist, men will support a coercive government, institution, or charismatic leader who can maintain harmony.

If a power vacuum is created, then the individuals motivated by the desire for power will vie for control of the existing instruments of power.

> In any situation in which power has failed and is in abeyance, some individual is certain to take it, appropriating as much as he can. Often he will encounter others on the same search; then he must either conquer them or secure their adherence, usually by offering hope of a share of power in the structure he proposes to create.[14]

The instruments of power and processes available to individuals are diverse but they must confer authority by consent of the subordinated. He who possesses authority exercises power.

Power is exercised by individuals but is transmitted through institutions. Therefore, it is necessary to understand the structural characteristics of the institutions within a given society as well as the motivating forces of those who dominate the bureaucractic machinery.[15]

The individuals who control the institutions of transmission procure their positions of authority through *tradition, violence* or *popular support*. However, different kinds of institutions develop different types of leaders. Also, various cultural traditions create different kinds of leaders and leaderships roles.

Since Aristotle, those studying power have centered their attention upon the state. Weber diverged from this view in undertaking his now famous study of bureaucracies. C. Wright Mills argues that power is embodied in the institutions of a society and not in the individual power holders. He argues for an elitist analysis of power as opposed to the pluralistic position held and propagated by Robert Dahl and others. Just as social thinkers have not been able to agree upon a definitive concept of power, they have not been able to agree upon the prevailing structures of power within societies.

The reason for all this talk about power is that it is a relationship, and not a "thing." Like love, power finds its significance — its meaning and tragedy — in human relationships and personal values as well as in the causal relationships of science.

NOTES

1. Harold Lasswell, *Power and Personality* (New York, Viking Press, 1948): p. 20.
2. Harold Lasswell and Abraham Kaplan, *Power and Society* (New Haven, Yale University Press, 1950): p. 92.
3. William Barrett, *Irrational Man* (Garden City, Doubleday, 1958): p. 31.
4. Arnold M. Rose, *The Power Structure* (New York, Oxford University Press, 1967): p. 49.
5. Gordon Tullock, *Toward a Mathematics of Politics* (Ann Arbor, University of Michigan Press): 1967.
6. Bertrand Russell, *Power* (New York, W. W. Norton & Co., 1938): p. 254.
7. Russell, *Power*, p. 255.
8. Rollo May, *Power and Innocence* (New York, W. W. Norton & Co., 1972): pp. 121-122.
9. Quoted from E. E. Schattschneider: *The SemiSovereign People* by Peter Bachrach and Morton S. Baratz: Two faces of power. John R. Champlin, ed. *Power* (New York, Atherton Press, 1971): p. 122.

10. Ortega Y. Gasset, *Man and People*, Willard R. Trask, trans. (New York, W. W. Norton & Co., 1957): p. 120.
11. Y Ortega, *Man and People*, p. 120.
12. Seymour M. Lipset, *Political Man* (Garden City, Doubleday, 1960): p. 8.
13. Adolf A. Berle, *Power* (New York, Harcourt, Brace & World, 1967): p. 39.
14. Berle, *Power*, p. 40.
15. Wolfgang Mommsen, Weber's Philosophy of History and Politics. Dennis Wrong, ed., *Max Weber*. Englewood Cliffs, Prentice-Hall, 1970): pp. 184-185.

2

THE PARADOX OF POWER

Roy Fairfield

"The closer you are to the center of power, the less you've got."

WHETHER this statement is original with me or was first made by somebody else, I do not know. But its germ of wisdom becomes increasingly clear. Perhaps the most timely illustration in modern history is that of Richard Nixon, prisoner of the very power he espoused and practiced; boxed in the very trap he seems to have set for himself. Max Weber points out how men with charisma, once in positions of power, move to bureaucratize their governments, their lives, their every move ... hence they become slaves of the system. Note the political lives of Nkrumah and Nehru. Men of charisma, paradoxically enough, have more power *before* they become responsible for daily decisions, *before* their work is tested by accountability criteria. In a United States, those criteria might relate to the Constitution, or "democratic" constituencies. In a Ghana or an India, emerging as nations in the mid-twentieth century, those criteria would be very much related to promises of freedom and the "revolution of rising expectations."

My colleague, Benjamin F. Thompson, frequently remarks, "He who has a *program* has no life of his own" — another vital angle of vision in perceiving the paradox of power. If one submerges all, or *even most* of one's energies into a program, project or promise, even law enforcement, then a person is likely to forget the very nature of his own being. True, programs, religions and causes may find nurture in the blood of the martyrs or the sweat of the founding fathers and mothers; true, a person may actualize himself by submerging but at what cost? And with what kind of power? Any systematic analysis of this phenomenon would have to come to grips with the truth behind the oft-seen poster, "When you're up to your ass in alligators, you forget you came to drain the swamp!"

During the past decade I frequently have found myself surrounded by alligators, many of them nourished by me! Having
been a founding father and director/coordinator of at least two
university-without-walls graduate programs, I have had the
power to assist in freeing students to learn in nontraditional
modes. But I have often asked myself, "Have I become a slave to
freeing students?" The paradox of power! Dedicated law enforcement officers, working the proverbial twenty-five hour day, must
be struck by the paradox and irony of enslaving themselves to
such regimens in order that citizens may freely walk down the
street or go to bed at night without fear of mayhem.

Formal and Informal

Most analytical discussions of power start by distinguishing
between formal and informal power. Suffice it to say here, formal
power is normally perceived as the power of a given office or role
in which the perimeters are outlined by guideposts, constitutions,
job descriptions, history, and continual operational processes.
On the other hand, informal power, whether in social, economic
or political terms, is that of the influences: Andrew Jackson's
Kitchen Cabinet or Franklin D. Roosevelt's trust; Jack Kennedy's
Brain trust; the card-playing buddy of the corporation president;
the wife or husband of many a great man or woman. Usually
informal power is wielded behind the scenes and sometimes is not
even discovered until a person leaves office or his memoirs are
published.

Yet whether one is concerned with formal power or informal
power, is there enough focus on the *paradox* of power? Could a
Saul Alinsky afford to admit that his power manipulations are
guaranteed to effect change for only the briefest moment? It is
always easy enough to find the enemy *without*, but what person
following the Alinsky model can see far enough to agree sooner or
later with Walt Kelley's Pogo that "We've met the enemy and they
is us?" Can a Marxist or Marxist type, seeking security in the
structure of social and logical dialectic, stand back far enough
from history to admit that today's oppressed become tomorrow's

oppressors? Can the man or woman with a powerful ego avoid the self-blinding power of ego long enough to understand that the wisest person is the one who doesn't let ego get in the way of perception?

Other paradoxes: those who would control the world through some kind of behavior modification — subliminal advertising, public relations mills, man-in-the-maze experiments — might consider whether or not humans would remain human for further modification if such power were successful. George Orwell in *1984,* Aldous Huxley in *Brave New World,* and other negative utopians have etched the dimensions of this puzzle; and even B. F. Skinner's *Walden II* raised the haunting specter long before he wrote *Beyond Freedom and Dignity.* One must also observe that the power brokers on Madison Avenue, drug pushers in the Mafia, and others who would power us toward lotus-eating may have already taken us to the point of no return — if we may judge true what Aldous Huxley said in his *Brave New World Revisited.* When he wrote *Brave New World,* he though it might take humans six hundred years to yield; twenty-five years later, during which *1984* was written, he conceded that we were almost there!

But let us look for a moment at positive utopias. They have not had a very sanguine history in this country. A few, such as the Oneida Community, have been successful in one way or another, but most have been ground into extinction by competition and other establishment forces. It's the old story of David and Goliath, or, more accurately, David and Leviathan! During the past decade, various counterculture members and some ecologically inclined persons have taken a kind of power into their own hands by founding various kinds of communities, or by returning to the land to humanize their lives. But all too frequently they are slow to realize that the minute they utilize the elements of the infrastructure (telephone, interstate highways, credit cards, etc.), they have forfeited their power. While their efforts should be judged by intensity rather than longevity, do they laugh at the paradox in their dilemma? I am reminded of a former student who came into my home to condemn just about everything I was doing even though he slept in my guest room, used my electricity, ate my food, used my telephone. As he was about to leave, he asked,

"Which way to Interstate 70?" I laughed, pointed out the paradox and suggested that he might return to his Eastern commune via the backroads of Ohio, New York, and Pennsylvania!

Pictures in the Mind

The American school system does much to perpetuate delusions of grandeur. Teachers tell Jimmy and Donna they must defer gratification if they want to grow up, gain power, earn big salaries, command respect (another paradox: *command* respect), and so on. Hence, most students know that they must be able to reproduce the pictures which the teacher has in her/his mind. And, of course, the Big Picture is the gold ring of power: President of the United States, senator, mayor, governor, the man in the big house, the woman with the big bank account who may even control the bank, the school, and the mayor! Culture heroes are generally rich, even sports figures: TV visually helps perpetuate that picture in the mind. Hence, Jimmy and Donna may fulfill another paradox: namely, achieving power by being obedient to some of the most powerful "ideals" of American life; be competitive, even ruthless if necessary, to get to the top of the ladder. So is it any wonder that a Richard Nixon could "make it" as king of the hill? After all, he was strong, male, sexist, and racist; he was a come-from-behind crisis-overcomer, the very model-syndrome which school officials tell us is the "promise of American life." And is it any wonder that those of us who pointed out the paradox — Nixon (the near-dictator) powering this "free" system — were treated as any prophet is in his own country? Who in the law and order business could deal with Nixon's violation of the law and creation of public confusion even as he mouthed platitudes about law and order? Yet there were many among us struggling to reconcile the paradoxes by claiming that "Yes and No" might be equally "true," who found comfort in Erich Fromm's discussion of "the pathology of normalcy in the *Sane Society*. By refusing to believe all of the pictures in the minds of Madison Avenue, our teachers, and TV, maintained the inner power of self-conviction, conviction that we were at least still alive, and had not become some trained Alpha or Beta of our strange new world.

T. S. Mathews, author and journalist, recently wrote a tribute to Edmund Wilson, perhaps America's most brilliant and influential twentieth century critic. Toward the end of his commentary, Mathews remarked,

> He was . . . a great American sage. He embodied that rare combination of stubborn skepticism, inveterate innocence, and sturdy, clarifying common sense that we used to consider peculiarly American — almost an American invention — but whose exponents now are sunk under the horizon, as deep as Atlantis. Wilson's sort, if it has not quite vanished from America, is the fast-dwindling, miniscule minority: although once dominant in the Republic's affairs, this old American type is now almost completely disfranchised and disregarded.[1]

Yes it is true, and perhaps because too many Americans have "bought into" somebody else's views of power. Too many are willing to maintain the "innocence" and let others provide the pictures. Too many cannot tolerate the disease of yes-no "truths" in paradoxical situations. We all learned that during the Watergate trials when thousands of Americans screamed for the return of their soap operas, or saved their faces as Nixon-lovers by claiming, "The situation is too complicated for me." Surely, Nixon, Haldeman, Ehrlichmann, Mitchell, and all of their bewildering sleights of hand were never in those pictures teachers showed us in school!

The Mystique of Power

Surely founding fathers such as Alexander Hamilton and James Madison were not that naive! As their cogently written *Federalist Papers* say so frequently, human passion and self-interest obstruct power organized for the public will. They repeatedly point out in the *Federalist* that the United States Constitution must check the dire effects of raw power passionately wielded through factional pressures. Hence, nobody should be trusted; well, almost nobody, for Hamilton in *Essay 78* does perceive the Supreme Court as a paper tiger who would guard the judiciary gates. But the genius of Hamilton's and Madison's viewpoint pivots around arguing, very much as Adam Smith had in the *Wealth of Nations,* that the total mechanism of checks and balances — geographically, economically, representationally, and so on — would somehow or other produce free government. And somehow or other, *almost* mysteriously, by hook or crook, by good planning and bad, by dint of vast natural and human resources, by some combination of belief in Manifest Destiny and stumble-bumble political accident, we have probably experienced *more* freedom rather than less in this country, even though one regrets what European whites did to limit the freedoms of native Americans, blacks, Chicanos and every other manner of minority. One could argue, as Reinhold Niebuhr does so brilliantly in the *Irony of American History* that we got where we are as much from our failures as from our successes. As so frequently observed about the Allies' victory over Hitler in World War II, "We made fewer mistakes." One could argue the case that when it came to dealing with the paradoxes of power involving the subtleties of human destruction we had failed with distinction! Though recognizing our vaunted technological successes (which may, in terms of survival, turn out to be failures) and the hopes they hold out for Third World Peoples, I cringe when I hear Africans and Asians talking about emulating our powerful way of harnessing natural and human resources to effect a more equitable way of life. I do not wish to deny them better diet, more creature comforts, less burdensome work conditions, more leisure, and so on, I merely wonder if they know what they are "buying" when they accept Western power concepts to effect that end.

Change Parameters

So, according to my angle of vision, we are naive to accept for our own lives the pictures in others' minds, naive in our failure to recognize the poisoning impact of power's mystique, and ostriches if we would accept simplistic analysis of power. I would further contend that one gains power, formally or informally, at the expense of power to shape oneself. Even sapiential authority (and one must learn to distinguish between the various kinds of *authority* which one may or may not have!) which depends heavily upon what one knows, can be deceptive if one takes oneself too seriously. It would seem to be a fact of power that to obtain it, one has to buy into the systems, values, objectives, terminology, and so on, of *others'* making. While one may have a hand in the shaping, there must be acceptance by another person of one's own person (to the nth degree if one wishes to control millions of dollars or people) if one wishes to effect control. Ironically, and/or paradoxically, to control or gain power over others, one must *submit* to the control of others. Those who seek power may *know* that; but, when "fame is the spur" or becoming rich is the objective, knowing is lost to feeling. Hence, one yields a bit of oneself here, another bit there, and so on.

One so frequently hears the rhetoric of *would-be changers.* The Alinskys would change the social structure with one method. Paolo Friere would use another. Revolutionists would do it quickly; revisionists are willing to take a little longer. Radicals might do it rapidly or slowly, so long as it gets done. Liberals, like the English, would muddle through with talk and legislation. But no matter what the tactic, the strategy is to effect change. And no matter the tactic or strategy, we are dealing with those who want power.

Having over the course of the past decade listened to every stripe of change agent seemingly known to humans, I am always amazed by the true-believer psychology; namely the change agent as authority, 99 times out of 100, knows that change is something *the other person* must do! That person also determines the criteria for judging, even in a *free* society!

Standards are weights the other person carries. And, indeed, there are no doubt billions of events, both small and large, in which a change agent *with might,* or even charisma, has altered the face of the globe, or at least part of it. Adolph Hitler illustrates one kind of might; Christ, Mohammed, and Gandhi reflect another. But, one wonders and speculates: Isn't there a profound irony in the fact that the change agent with *the* truth may as frequently destroy others as save them? To paraphrase the fabulist, William March: Wouldn't humankind have been saved long ago if it had not been for its saviors? Naturally, it's not a simple analysis of good and evil; nothing ever is! One can argue that Hitler saved the sanity of many Germans just as Christ and

Gandhi offered hope to many oppressed persons. Yet one can argue the evil side too; namely, Hitler obviously triggered the ruination of hundreds of millions of people just as secular and religious leaders, led by greed, twisted the teachings of Christ and Mohammed to promote "holy wars." So, the question remains: can change agents, who hope to effect social, political or economic (to say nothing about spiritual or human) change, using some powerful vehicle, *be permitted* to let their power loose — *if* they are unwilling to change themselves? And yet who would have the power to do the permitting? or stop them if they have the might to override the permit? Also, who will give these change agents the paradox test; namely, test them to see if their sense of paradox of power prepares them for wheeling and dealing in power? And if they do not pass the paradox test because their paradox quotient is low, under what circumstances will they maintain their citizenship, their membership, or their humanness?

Less speculative perhaps, but no less important, is the need for general acceptance and new perception of the extent to which anybody in a position of power can change anything. Again, let us look at the Presidency of the United States. As so many analyses of that institution make "perfectly clear," the President has enormous power; yet, his power to *change* the characteristic elements of his office is not always as great as is commonly perceived by the American populace. Surely, as one looks at acceleration in the accumulation of power, from Franklin Roosevelt to Gerald Ford, one sees the total leap as having quantum proportions. Nixon got very close to stealing the country! But, the oft-expressed hope that a change of administration will effect a change in power proportions is clearly an illusion — if not a delusion — when the voter steps into the booth to record his option for a favorite candidate. Even the much-vaunted new federalism or decentralization of power in the United States is paced by Washington! In short, the momentum of power, either in the Presidency or in any other branch of American government — local, state or national — tends to move in a single direction. Hence, in a very real and historically verifiable sense, those closest to the center of power often have very little power *to change its direction.* In many senses this is a more complex and more profound paradox than the notion that the closer one is to the center of power the less power one has to bring about ends which that person wishes to effect. Those authorities who promise "law and order" in our time may well ponder these several paradoxes, individually or in concert with their fellow and sister promisers.

Psychology and Politics

In many senses the paradox of power is really central to the human condition. Humans are the only creatures who *know* they are going to die; yet, they frequently act as though they were going to live forever. Humans know they "can't take it with them," yet they seek status, power, and wealth, and in that process kill themselves, either metaphorically or physically, thereby guaranteeing that they will not take it with them! Humans will "buy" fetishes, myths, illusions, power, religions, nostrums, etc., *ad infinitum* and in the "buying" create the will to believe in those fetishes, myths, illusions, power, religions, nostrums, and so on, *ad infinitum!* Humans will also invent ideologies that they insist others must believe, some of which are replete with paradox, such as, "Fight for peace, or I'll kill you." At some U. S. Air Force bases, one is greeted with the motto, "Peace is our business," and Barry Goldwater advocates force to keep the peace. In short, the human condition is filled with paradox; yet, few politicans and few political scientists seem to link psychology and politics in this fundamental way. Of course, one might sardonically add: if they did, they probably would not get elected to public office or become full professors and consultants!

No doubt about it, American public life is notoriously short of psychologists or philosophers with cosmic vision — or much sense of *humans in the universe*. While we have had several presidents capable of a philosophical viewpoint or two, it might be argued that we have had only a philosopher or two; maybe Jefferson and Wilson? In a society as pragmatic and expedient as ours, the presidency may be no place for philosophers or men of vision. Congress, too, has had mighty few, maybe countable on both hands and feet if one stretches the concept a bit. Nor can the

Supreme Court boast of more than a handful, legal training and Anglo-American judicial processes virtually guaranteeing that! Nor could one find many persons in state and local governments to populate a Pantheon for the philosophically courageous! Hence, it may be too much to ask public officials to "buy" into concern for and action upon notions related to the paradox of power.

But, is it too much to ask intelligent Americans, a healthy segment of the American people, to become more aware of the many manifestations of power and the consequences of ignoring such paradoxes as those alluded to here? Can those concerned about their own humanness ignore a mindless approach to power, power at any cost, power at the expense of sensitivity, power at the expense of destroying both self and others? Can anybody sensitive to the "power corrupts and absolute power corrupts absolutely" dictum not wonder how that might affect him or her? Can Freud be so right about the death wish that so-called "healthy" humans can overlook the insight in the view-point that "in ideology there is death"?

I have frequently remarked that education will not be successful until it facilitates the development of children and adults in appreciating self in the context of irony, paradox, and humor. That's a *big* task! And until educators and parents of the world are able to do just that, perhaps we can only hope that would-be dictators, authoritarians, and the power-hungry in any walk of life can be teased into laughing so hard at others that they'll laugh themselves to death — or at least into a powerless state!

NOTES

1. T. S. Mathews: "Edmund Wilson: An American Original," *Saturday Review* 2:23, 1975.

3

THE PROBLEM OF POWER*

Michel Crozier

ANY crisis that paves the way for or accompanies a profound change in society forces us to come to grips with the basic problem in all collective life: the problem of power.

In recent years protesters have focused on the problem of authority rather than on the problem of power.[1] But if authority — traditional or legal authority — were to be weakened, or even if it were to collapse, it does not necessarily follow that human relations would suddenly become free and transparent. The moment an old legitimacy, in which even its possessors have lost faith, is seriously challenged, new power phenomena begin to emerge that cannot be ignored without creating irresistible pressure for a return to the old forms.

For a long time, the popularity of Marxism and the violence of the antagonisms it aroused prevented us from seeing the importance of this problem in a society that had already changed profoundly, and was perhaps ripe for further change. In the heat of a more and more anachronistic debate — its terms of reference were all nineteenth-century ones — we let ourselves be carried away with the idea that the problem of power was secondary to more essential issues, such as those of property or development, of which it was no more than an instrument or justification. But the internal crisis which many of our institutions are now experiencing gives us some idea of the primacy of problems of government in its broadest sense — the organization of power relationships among men.

The more we recognize the fragility of the old order based on nothing more than conventions, and thus discover how free we really are to create a new order, the more we are obliged to recognize that we cannot escape dealing with this problem, that we

*Reprinted from *Social Research*, vol. 40 2 (New York, N.Y.: New School for Social Research), page 211-28, with permission of the publisher.

absolutely must try to find a means of regulating power relationships among people, and that all other problems are merely the conditions or consequences of this fundamental issue. Simplistic propositions and fanatical demands which blossom forth on all sides in the midst of the present crisis do not falsify this analysis if we see them for what they are: In the face of anxiety created by awareness of our freedom, they are panic responses and desperate attempts to rediscover the security of clear-cut distinctions.

Can the social sciences enable us to deal more positively with the disturbing problem of power? They too are profoundly marked by the customs and taboos of an era when a great deal of time was spent trying to avoid the issue. But it is only in their terms, and through their renewal, that we can identify and state the problem of power in its entirety. Above all, it is through work now being done by social scientists that we can assess the kinds of progress made possible by evolution, and judge man's capacity to develop better arrangements for dealing with power in the future.

The Social-Science Difficulties

The concept of power is central to the social sciences. Phenomena of power always accompany all processes of social integration, and these are one of the subjects, if not the essential subject, of study in sociology. One might even say that, without power, neither integration nor society is possible. But since the social sciences are not very fully developed, and consequently reflect very closely the prejudices of their time, they are ill prepared to use this kind of concept effectively.

The concept of power is, in fact, extremely difficult to deal with. It is too vague and too ambiguous, and it too easily explains too many problems. Worse, it is difficult to clarify it, since its imprecision, and the contraditions it raises, stem not from the uncertainty of the word "power," but from the ambiguity of the facts of power themselves.

Sociologists and political scientists have long been wary of difficulties of this kind. Empirically oriented sociologists, influenced by a rather narrow kind of scientism, have nearly always claimed that they disregard phenomena that are too imprecise or that cannot be quantified; they study the determinants of attitudes and behavior as though the only kinds of relationships that existed between people were formal ones, or phenomena of spontaneous attraction. The more classical, humanist sociologists would seem, on the contrary, to have projected the systematic interpretive schemas they could not develop elsewhere onto this confused subject — hence the flowering of conspiracy theories of power (such as C. Wright Mills'), and theories of the absence or universal distribution of power. But fascination with power as a myth turns out to be no more constructive than the empiricists' neglect. Withal, the two attitudes would appear complementary.

To get over these contradictions, one must squarely face a spot that all the perfumes of our ideological Arabias cannot sweeten: No concrete relationship between either individuals or groups can be free of issues of power.

In the last few years social scientists have made some progress here. We are gradually learning to approach the issue experimentally, thanks in part to the development of new disciplines like decision-making theory and games theory, and to the influence they have had on political science and sociology, and in part to greater empirical understanding of the sociology of organizations. Here the theoretical and empirical efforts join in trying to state the problems of government in concrete, if not yet operational, terms. But the new approach nonetheless raises several important questions. The awkwardness and contradictions surrounding power phenoma can only be dissipated gradually, and this is so for three very different reasons: moral, logical, and methodological.

From the moral point of view, it is still very hard to rid ourselves of all the moral taboos that have grown up around this subject. Everyone claims to be liberated in this respect, but this freedom is usually no more than a suppression of the problem. The taboo about power is still perhaps more profoundly rooted in the conscience of modern man than the taboo about sex. The right-thinking modern intellectual, who is horrified when one speaks of sexual behavior in terms of good and evil, is deeply shocked by any scientific analysis of relations of dependence or domination. For him and for most of us, domination and dependence are moral categories, not facts.

From the point of view of logic, power phenomena, because they are integrative, arise naturally from contradictory and at first view irreconcilable modes of reasoning. To understand them one must pursue both a rational, instrumental analysis of the classic type and an affective type of analysis at the same time. Indeed, power can be conceived only in an ends-oriented perspective, which suggests that the power game must always conform, in one way or another, to rational rules based on efficiency; but at the same time it arouses some extremely strong affective reactions, so that the play of power is also conditioned by the capacity of individuals to withstand these reactions.

Lastly, from a structural point of view, no power relationship can be dissociated from the institutional system or systems within which it develops. There can be no neutral field. Each power relationship is shaped by a whole series of "structural" constraints that condition the rules of the game, and it therefore expresses, at a secondary level, the logic of the institutions or structures. However autonomous it may be, it cannot change substantially without deeply affecting the system of which it is an integral part.

Faced with these obstacles, social scientists have too often let their work dwindle into description or only partial analysis. For example, they will make distinctions among types of power according to the way it is exercised: power based on coercion, power based on the distribution of rewards or on mechanisms of identification, power based on expertise, and legitimate power. This way of going about it may be useful as a start, but it immediately stumbles on a huge block: It gives us no help in understanding how different types of power are reconciled and how arbitration between them operates. The principal virtue of power as an integrative phenomenon is that it is susceptible to confrontation, transfer, and exchange. If one claims that forms of power coming from different sources have nothing in common and cannot be compared, then it is impossible to understand or predict how, in reality, they are brought together and how they balance each other out. Let us take an example. The legitimate power a mayor has over the municipal employees subordinate to him is clearly completely different from the kind of power that private interests who could bribe them, or the network of relationships they depend on to do their work efficiently, may have over these same employees. Obviously, these various forms of power exercised over the same group of people are different in kind, and it is important not to confuse them. We must distinguish clearly between them, and even oppose them for analytical purposes. But it is also essential that we discover their common denominator in order to understand the results of their interaction.

We must therefore go beyond the descriptive approach, which is mainly of taxonomic interest, in order, if possible, to lay the empirical foundations of a "strategic" analysis that will enable us to assess the opposing forces, and to uncover the laws governing their interaction and reconciliation.

This can be achieved, I believe — or at least we can make a start — if we no longer consider power solely from the viewpoint of a "wielder" of power, but look on it rather as a relationship between individuals or groups, as a process developing over time that, with its goals and its rules of play, affects the organization or system within which the various parties act (or which they have formed for the purpose).

Power as a Relationship and as a Process

Any kind of power, whatever its sources, its legitimacy, objectives, and means whereby it is exercised, implies the possibility of action by an individual or group on one or more other individuals or groups. This is what Robert Dahl wanted to make clear when he proposed his famous, oft-quoted definition: "The power of A over B is the capacity of A to make B do something he would not have done without the intervention of A."

The main virtue of a definition like this is its simplicity. It has the advantage that it does not require as a prerequisite any theory about the essence of power, it is equally applicable to all forms of power, and it makes power amenable to some sort of measurement. But if one wants to use it operationally, it presents some difficulties.

In the first place, it does not really enable us to distinguish between power as an intentional, conscious relationship, which implies a confrontation between two parties, and power as an involuntary influence that one actor may exert over another without either of them necessarily being aware of it. Clearly we can speak of power in both cases, but equally clearly we are not speaking about the same thing.

In the second place, precise measurement is not very likely, since A's capacity to exercise power over B varies depending on the action demanded, and experience shows that there is no standard of measurement. Each "power relation" is specific: A can make B do "a," whereas X, who cannot make B do this, can, on the other hand, get him to do "b," which A couldn't possibly manage.

Lastly, and most important, experience has shown us that a "power relation" is not only specific but also reciprocal; if A can make B do something he would not have done otherwise, it is quite likely that B, for his part, is capable of making A do something he would not have done without B's intervention.

These difficulties need not stop us from using Dahl's definition, but they do limit its applicability to relatively vague comparisons bearing solely on the capacities of each individual as a wielder of power. This kind of comparison lets us emphasize the universal and interchangeable nature of power relations, but it tells us little about the way they work.

If we take a look now, not at power in the sense of the individual capacity of A and B, but at the power that develops in relations between the two parties A and B, we discover a bargaining element that completely alters the meaning of the thing. Any relationship between two parties requires a measure of exchange and mutual adjustment. Any positive response by A to a request by B may clearly be considered to be the consequence of B's power over A. But it is simpler, and more fruitful, to look at it rather as the result of negotiation. A responds to B's demands because B has responded to A's, or else because A thinks B will respond to him. If the two parties are completely free and if the exchange is equal, one cannot really talk in terms of power. But if the balance of the exchange is tipped one way or the other, and if this inequality corresponds to the respective situations of the two parties and is not the result of chance or an error on the part of one of them, then we can speak of a power relationship. We can then justifiably say, somewhat altering Dahl's original statement, that A's power over B corresponds to A's capacity to impose on B terms of exchange that are favorable to him.

If one accepts this new formulation, the essential problem of power is no longer that of the capacity for command or action, but the more precise and limited problem of the conditions governing interaction between partners.

At first sight, it might seem as though the relative strength of the two parties — the balance of power — would naturally determine the outcome. But this proposition has no operational value, since strength and balance of power are only meaningful in terms of the relationship itself. Strong people are not strong in the abstract. They must be both willing and able to exercise their strength. In a situation where the use of force or wealth is either forbidden or impossible, the weak and poor can prevail over the rich and strong; the balance of power thus becomes the balance of pertinent and usable power.

The analysis is now somewhat more precise, but it is still inadequate, for it tells us nothing about the nature of the forces or about the players' strategy. Strength and power cannot be accumulated like war chests. If we observe the players closely, we see that the key to their behavior lies in the margin of freedom and of maneuver they can secure for themselves. A confrontation between partners is not a trial of strength, but an exchange of possibilities of action. Let us take the rare but not unusual case of a powerful executive who is restricted when dealing with a weak subordinate to a single possible course of action, while the subordinate can choose among several. The executive will have nothing to exchange and will be in an inferior position vis-à-vis the subordinate — who can, if he keeps a cool head, cause him serious difficulties. The more one can affect one's partner's situation by using one's freedom of maneuver, the less vulnerable one is before him and the more power one has over him. The game consists, then, in trying to force the other player into a determinate pattern of behavior while at the same time staying free enough oneself to be able to make him pay for one's goodwill. The balance of power is a confrontation between the partners' respective abilities to keep their future behavior less predictable than their adversary's.

Strength, wealth, prestige, legitimate authority are influential only insofar as they give their possessors greater freedom of action.

In the context of a simple bargaining relationship, however, notions of freedom of action and predictability of behavior are vague. They can be made more precise only if we put this relationship in its natural context, i.e., a more or less structured system, with its own manifest and latent objectives and its own rules.

Power does not exist in a vacuum. A power relation can only develop if the two parties are already part of, or choose to participate in, an organized system, however temporarily. Two strangers meeting in a railway carriage do not find themselves in a power situation, regardless of any cultural differences or inequalities in strength or wealth. But the moment circumstances join them together in a common undertaking, the negotiations they are implicitly forced to engage in will reveal the development of a power relationship, the start of an organization. The terms of exchange and the conditions of the negotiation are in fact profoundly linked to their joint enterprise, and in a certain sense express it. Power requires organization. Men can attain their collective ends only through the exercise of power relationships, but, conversely, they can exercise power over each other only when pursuing these collective ends, which directly condition their bargaining activities.

To understand the basic elements and dynamics of power negotiations, one must focus on the overall organization serving as their framework. Power then appears no longer merely as a relationship, but as a process inseparable from the organizational process. The terms of the exchange result neither from chance nor from some abstract and theoretical balance of power. They are the result of a game whose constraints create compulsory hurdles and opportunities for manipulation for the players, and therefore determine their strategy.

What are these constraints? Basically, they are the formal and informal objectives laid down by the organization and accepted by the participants, as well as the rules imposed on them or established by them. We should emphasize that these objectives and these rules do not work directly. Their principal role is indirect: By limiting the players' freedom of action they will establish sectors where actions are entirely predictable, and others where uncertainty dominates.

In negotiating with the organization, a player's power ultimately depends on the control he has over a source of uncertainty that affects the pursuit of the organization's aims, and on the importance of this source as compared with other relevant sources. In negotiating with another player, his power depends on the control he can exercise over a source of uncertainty affecting this other player's behavior within the context of the rules imposed by the organization.

To go further, we must resort to case-study analyses. To measure one individual's power over another, one must analyze the sources of uncertainty each controls within the organization they belong to, the respective importance of these uncertainties to the organization's objectives, and the limitations imposed on both players by the rules they must obey in order to continue playing. We have come a long way from the usual mechanical models and those famously clever but contradictory axioms about power ("The more one demonstrates power the more one acquires it"; "The more one exercises one's power the weaker it becomes"[2]), yet this institutional approach precludes neither the measurement of phenomena nor the search for more general laws. However, insistence on their insertion into a structural study makes such attempts extremely difficult. In particular, the problem of rules constitutes a preliminary problem that cannot easily be resolved.

The Two Faces of Power

Each participant in an organization, in an organized system, or even in society as a whole, wields power over the system he belongs to and over the members of this system, insofar as he occupies a strategically favorable position as regards the problems on which the success of the system depends. But at the same time, his power is limited by the rules of the game, which restrict the use he can make of his advantages.

However, while it may be natural enough to begin by separately studying, first, the mechanism of power relationships arising out of the explicit and implicit bargains that individuals strike between themselves and with the organization, and, second, the rules preventing the players from using their advantages beyond a certain point, an analysis more attentive to reality would lead us to look on the second factor, the rules themselves, as a crystallization of other power relationships and the results of earlier negotiations which may have been less explicit but were every bit as real. The rules of the game tend, in effect, to demarcate artificial sources of uncertainty, enabling those who control them to negotiate on better terms with players whose favorable strategic situation otherwise puts them in a position of superiority. Moreover, the rules can develop and gain acceptance only because another source of uncertainty, more important than all the others — namely, the question of the survival of the entire organization — binds all of its members.

This analysis may seem unduly formal, but it serves the important purpose of highlighting two contradictory aspects of power that are indissolubly linked together. On the one hand, the power relationship appears as something inadmissible and shameful — quite simply, as blackmail. On the other hand, power is honored as the legitimate, necessary, and respectable expression of the social control that is vital to the success of any collective effort. It might be argued that this contrast is unwarranted, and depends on an arbitrarily extensive definition of power. But this objection will not stand up to close scrutiny, for the official pyramid of power cannot operate without recourse to blackmail, while in all informal negotiations based on blackmail, social constraints, the general interest, and the primacy of collective goals still have some part to play.

Let us take the example of the relations between superiors and subordinates within an organization. The superior has the right to give certain orders to his subordinates, while the latters' duty is to obey these orders. This relationship is highly valued, and it retains a moral connotation, in our vocabulary at least: We still speak of the *duty* to obey, and we are still morally shocked by insubordination, which we can only explain in terms of moral failing on the part of one or the other of the protagonists. On the other hand, if the superior uses his preeminence to obtain something from his subordinates that is not provided for in the rules, we then speak of an abuse of power. In reality, however, the two go together. Subordinates are in a position to exert a great deal of pressure on their boss, since his success in an organization ultimately depends on their zeal and goodwill. He can respond to these pressures only by "abusing" his power. He must, in order to retain sufficient freedom of maneuver, threaten to apply the rules strictly and, conversely, make it understood that he will tolerate substantial stretching of the rules in exchange for good behavior; if he depended solely on his legitimate power, he would quickly find himself powerless. In contrast, the expert who knows that he is irreplaceable and who could theoretically, therefore, blackmail the organization into accepting almost anything, can only use official procedures and must make it clear that he subscribes to the common goals of the organization. He cannot succeed in manipulating the organization unless he lets himself be manipulated by it. In both cases, the shameful and the noble faces of power are inextricably bound together. Blackmail is employed for lofty ends, and noble power serves as a screen for blackmail operations.

I have wittingly used moral terms here because common sense and sociology are agreed that moral judgments are definitely involved: Power is good and noble if it corresponds to the officially accepted social pact; it is reprehensible and immoral if it is used as a means to take advantage of one's situation in order to manipulate others outside the recognized pact. But experience makes it clear that moral judgments of this kind are contradictory, for power in its noble aspect arises out of dubious negotiations, and has to rely on blackmail in its exercise. The established order of things is merely the ratified outcome of prior relationships in which blackmail played a major role. On what grounds can we condemn present blackmail in the name of past ones? It is anyway impossible to eliminate blackmail, since it is related to the perennial need for adjustment and innovation. No human enterprise can adapt to its environment if it is reduced to its formal power, to the theoretical pact which defines it.

As is frequently the case in such matters, judgments become more violent as the distinction between good and evil becomes more dubious. This may be one of the reasons why the concept of power remains so ambiguous, and why sociologists have such difficulty using it.

All the same, the critique made by traditional morals would be of little interest if it did not reveal the function of this moralism and how it can be overcome. The value we attribute to power in the noble sense of the term derives, I believe, from the fact that all collective human undertakings have great difficulty in gaining the adherence and conformity of their participants. To impose the priority of collective goals over individual claims, the latter have to be considered morally reprehensible, while the official hierarchic power is, in contrast, exalted as the guardian of the collective goal. Negotiation is suppressed if it threatens to jeopardize the organized system that most of the participants believe to be indispensable, and moral or religious reasoning is invoked instead. Of course, even moral discussion involves pressures and counterpressures; we speak, for example, of a fair wage and of the necessary prerogatives of the leader. Only little by little can the real nature of human relations be talked about openly, as people become readier to understand and accept the disciplines necessary to collective action. I would like to argue that the major trend in organization practice over the past hundred years has been one from the rule of morality to the rule of negotiation.

If we can extrapolate from the experience of organizations to the functioning of broader, less structured entities, we can say that this gradually emerging consciousness on the part of societies constitutes a new kind of coming of age — comparable to earlier awakenings concerning, for example, anthropocentrism and ethnocentrism.

The clearest example of this evolution, and the one most easy to acknowledge because it has been established for so long, is the recognition of the right to strike. Few people now recall that strikes were once considered an unthinkable form of blackmail and that they only gradually came to be accepted as a legitimate form of the power to negotiate. This evolution is far from complete, but we can clearly see the direction it is taking.

The gradual recognition of reality and of the legitimacy of each participant's use of his advantages in collective life is a sign of greater maturity among individuals and of their organizational capacities in a given society. But at the same time it completely alters the conditions of collective action. The impulses which before could only be expressed in contradictions and paralyses of bureaucracies or hierarchies, in religious and social taboos, can now be resolved more rapidly and efficiently. Hierarchical power need depend less on constraint, and can divest itself of its problematical moral attributes in favor of greater flexibility and effectiveness, playing the less prestigious role of inspirer and facilitator.

This is a very different kind of evolution from what is hoped for in anarchist and revolutionary demands for the withering away of power. The general acceptance of open negotiation does not signify the elimination of power; on the contrary, it implies the rational acceptance of all *de facto* powers. It tends to reintegrate formerly shameful practices into the field of legitimate human relationships. It may seem paradoxical to view the disappearance of the traditional dichotomy between the official, rigid world of the formal hierarchy and the darker world of secret dealings as progress. But this change of perspective enables us to make human relations more wholesome in the same way that the rehabilitation of man's repressed drives by psychoanalysis helps him to be more free and more responsible. At the same time, shameful power practices become less so when legitimate power loses its halo of nobility, and when society, recognizing the pressures arising out of the natural interaction of its members, makes it easier for its members to participate in the achievement of society's goals. Change becomes natural and innovation is encouraged.

Power within the Social System

These few remarks concerning power as a social process, as a condition, and as an expression do not, of course, permit us to make any conclusions about the government of a social system. Nevertheless, they highlight a few basic points concerning the general evolution of power relationships in modern industrial and postindustrial societies.

Problems of power in society as a whole are not so simple as those in an organization. We have to deal with relationships on another level, carried on between organization, each having a specific rationale, far more determinate and settled than the rationality of the system within which their negotiations take place. Moreover, the games played by individuals, organizations, and society as a whole tend to overlap and coincide. Society can influence organizations through the pressure of individuals. And this brings us to the concept of influence, which we have so far ignored in our discussion of organizations, but which is decisively important here. It is through this type of power — unconscious, unnegotiated influence — that social control is exercised and that the rules of play permitting society as a whole to continue functioning are imposed, in the face of divergent pressures from all the different interests at stake.

These differences and oppositions do not, however, completely transform the situation. The rules we have established concerning the necessary link between all power relations and the beginning of an organized system with shared objectives and rules also apply to society as a whole. Negotiations in society are not free, nor do they correspond to any mechanical application of the balance of power. Rather, the balance of power depends essentially on constraints affecting all the parties involved and reflecting their relative dependence in society as a whole. As is the case within an organization, each party tries to manipulate this relationship by using what mastery it has over the sources of uncertainty affecting the other party's behavior, at the same time respecting the commonly accepted rules and objectives. The most important difference is that the countervailing power, the social control governing the whole, is not very formalized or constraining and must use much more indirect means. But all the same, a high moral value is placed on it, and if most of the time it cannot capitalize on the entire society's need to survive, it can nonetheless, in such extreme cases as war, appeal to this necessity.

These likenesses are becoming more and more important in the modern world, as the result of a double movement that is bringing organizations and society closer together. On the one hand, the fact that organizations are evolving toward more open and tolerant forms of human relationships is tending to transform them into "political societies." On the other hand, society as a whole is giving rise to organized subsystems, within which social control is expressed through more and more conscious decisions.

These two convergent phenomena may appear incompatible: more tolerance on one side, increasing rigor on the other. But, at a deeper level, they reflect the same evolution. We try to integrate into the formal decision-making procedure those unacknowledged negotiations which accompany and paralyze it. We also seek to substitute organized systems, which allow fully conscious decisions, for the blind conflict of interests, which can take no account of secondary consequences. The effort is being made in a number of realms, but on both sides the approach is much the same — people are realizing the complexity of action — and so is the objective: to broaden the accepted range of forces at play so that we can openly (and contradictorily) take into account both the interests and the strategic positions bearing on the situation, as well as the general interest of the surrounding milieu.

In the case of society as a whole, we are concerned not with the integration of a hidden world whose existence has hitherto been denied, but with bridging the deep chasm that separated the world of interests from the world of formal or moral decisions. The clearest aspect of this change — the recognition of the importance of interests in formal or moral decisions, and official consultation between powers whose concealed blackmail had hitherto been considered immoral — stems from precisely the same inspiration we have already noted in organizations. In both instances we have become more acutely aware of the conditions under which human beings participate in the collective enterprise, and a new, more tolerant vision of the relationship between the two faces — moral and immoral, noble and ignoble — of power. Moralization, tolerance, and rationalization go hand in hand.

One final problem remains to be dealt with, however — that of the general interest. We know that the general interest does not arise from the confrontation of all interests taken together, and that tolerance and acceptance of all those inadmissible pressures are not enough to produce a "general interest." Something more is needed, whereby the whole becomes more than the sum of its parts. In the case of an organization, the power corresponding to this need is attached to its leadership, which affirms it by using the uncertainty affecting all the members concerning the survival of the organization and their continued membership in it. In the case of society as a whole, no equivalent criterion enables us clearly to assess the general interest.

Hence the high moral value placed on politics, and the persistence of an unavoidable imperative factor. In the first place a state policy is the outcome of the play between diverse influences affecting individuals and the resulting consensus on the one hand, and on the other the pressures of all existing powers; but, in the second place, it depends on contingent choices made above and beyond this by leaders in strategic positions. In the dialogue between the leaders and the mass of society's members concerning what proportion of arbitrary power should be left in the hands of the former, the general interest can evolve from the metaphysical to the rational plane. This transformation is only now becoming possible. But its accomplishment depends far less on progress made in the conception or ideology of the general interest than it does on a healthy interplay of power relations. We cannot deal rationally with the irreducible element of freedom so long as we have failed to rationalize and moralize the preponderant element of functioning and constraint that conditions all activity.

NOTES

1. I shall distinguish here between the problem of authority — any form of power recognized as legitimate by law, custom, or a sufficient consensus of those subject to it — and the problem of power in general — that is, all relationships between men characterized by the phenomena of dependence, manipulation, or exploitation.
2. See James March, *The Power of Power*.

4

THE CONCEPT OF AUTHORITY

RICHARD T. DE GEORGE

THERE are many uses for the word *authority*; it has many meanings, and many different conceptions. Any theory of authority should consider these meanings and uses, and an adequate theory should account for them. Is there something they all have in common? Is there some root concept or general conception which includes the various conceptions as its subsidiaries? The history of social and political thought gives us several answers to this question, as do religious theories and commonsense views. But the answer should not be supplied dogmatically; it should evolve.

Let us start, therefore, simply by looking at some of the ordinary uses of the term "authority" to see if they throw any light on the concept. To describe varying uses settles nothing, but if, as a starting point, we can see whether there are discrepancies in use, we can get some idea of what different meanings are given to the term, and we can see where, and perhaps why, some tidying up or reforming of its definition may be useful.

For instance, we speak of someone being an authority on a certain topic, as when we say "Professor Jones is an authority on early American history." We speak of people being in authority, and such people are frequently referred to as "the authorities," as in "that crime should be reported to the authorities." People in authority are frequently said to have authority. Thus a justice of the peace will say "By the authority vested in me by the State of Kansas, I now pronounce you man and wife." People who have authority are sometimes said to have been authorized to do thus and so, and we can refer to "an authorized representative" or an "authorized dealer." We speak not only of people having, or exercising, or being authorities, but we also speak of things embodying authority, as when we refer to "the authority of the law," or when we point to a set of rules as being "the final authority in a game." People are said to speak with authority or to act authoritatively, and so on.

The phrase in which the word *authority* or some variant of it is used arises in certain contexts, and in many instances other words can be used instead. Sometimes we speak of the "person in authority," but at other times we might just as well refer to "the person in charge." A person who has the authority to perform certain acts might in some instances be said to have the right to perform those acts, or the power to act in such and such a way. A final authority might be a court of last appeal. Hence the use of the word *authority* should be taken as an index of what we are after. People displayed the characteristics of what has come to be called an "authoritarian personality" before that term was coined. Our concern should be not simply with the word, but with certain practices, actions, states of affairs, or conceptual schemes in which authority plays a role, and which can be described as involving authority — though some other word or phrase might be substituted for the word *authority* in many of its forms or derivatives.

Are there common characteristics which all forms of authority have or share? The answer can be arrived at only after we have established what kinds of authority exist. But even before turning our attention to some authority types, it will be useful to have a working model, or concept, of authority which can be modified in the light of further argument or future considerations.

Authority is primarily a relational concept. When we speak of a person being an authority, whether we mean that he is an authority on a certain topic, or whether we mean that he is a holder of a certain office or position, we relate him in certain ways to others, to a certain body of knowledge, to certain activities, or to something else of the kind.

To say "Professor Jones is an authority on early American history" is to say something not only about his knowledge on an absolute scale, but also about his knowledge relative to that of others. To be an expert on early American history is to have a great deal of detailed knowledge on the topic. To be an authority seems to say more; that is, not only does Professor Jones have a great deal of knowledge, but he is an authority in a social context, he is an authority for others who are either not expert or not as expert in his field. That someone can be an authority without there being someone for whom, at least potentially, he can be an authority, seems to be a misuse of the term. But whether or not it is so, the model which I shall initially propose takes the notion of authority when applied to a person to be a relational term; for it seems indubitable that there are certainly a large number of cases in which this is the case. The relationship is triadic, since it is between at least two people — one of whom is an authority. No one is an authority in general. He is always an authority in some specific realm or field. Thus, some X is an authority for some Y over some field or realm, as Professor Jones is an authority for his students in the field of early American history, or the judge in a courtroom is the authority for those in the courtroom over the proceedings of the trial in progress, or the boss is the authority for the secretary as to what letters she should type first in the office.

Notice, however, that not only is X an authority for Y over a certain field, but in certain cases it is appropriate to say that he exercises his authority, and sometimes he exercises it over Y. Now what is exercised is clearly different from the person who exercises it; and though sometimes a person is called an authority because he exercises authority over others, this is not necessarily the case. A teacher may be an authority for his students without exercising authority over them, or without exercising authority at all. It is even difficult in this case to say that he *has* authority rather than to say that he *is* an authority. Yet a judge in a courtroom might both be an authority and have authority, which he may or may not exercise. Authority as a noun may therefore designate some person who is an authority, or it may refer to what a person has which may make him an authority, or it may designate something exercised by someone, who may be an authority.

Now since we know that some people are authorities for others, we can identify them as *de facto* authorities; and since we know that some people exercise authority we can refer to the authority they exercise as *de facto* authority. This leaves open the question of whether it is ever right — according to some criteria or other — for one person to be an authority for another or for anyone to have or exercise authority. A variety of justifications have been given for people being authorities and for their exercising authority. The justifications consist of reasons which are given to justify practices of institutions. We can speak of the source of authority as the basis upon which such an argument or justification for authority rests; and we can call the grounds for authority the argument or justification itself. Thus it may be that though there is a source of authority, the grounds for the exercise of authority are not made out, or the case is poorly presented.

De facto authority (in reality) and a *de facto authority* can be distinguished from *de jure* authority (by right) and a *de jure* authority. The latter are instances of grounded authority, though whether or not any authority is grounded is still an open question. The notions of *de jure* and *de facto* authority as used here should not be confused with what I shall call legitimate and illegitimate authority. Legitimate authority is the authority obtained and exercised according to a certain set of rules or legal procedures; illegitimate authority is authority exercised within a legal framework or within the framework established by another set of rules, but not in accordance with the laws or rules. Authority may be legitimate but not grounded because the legal framework is not grounded or justified; and it may be illegitimate but grounded, which means justified though contrary to the rules or law. It is important to have both the pair legitimate-illegitimate and the pair *de facto-de jure* because there are two different distinctions to be made. If we try to make do with only the latter pair, legitimate authority might always be thought to be *de jure* and illegitimate authority *de facto*. But clearly *de facto* authority might be either legitimate or illegitimate. It should also be noted that *de facto* authority may also be *de jure*, that is grounded; but legitimate authority can never be illegitimate or vice-versa. Legitimate and illegitimate are opposites, while *de facto* and *de jure* are not.

An authority may be formally recognized according to some procedure — be it a licensing procedure, or the granting of a diploma or honorary degree — or he may be informally recognized, for instance, by his friends, or students, or neighbors. The authority he exercises may be formal or informal. It may also be effective or ineffective (as he may be an effective or ineffective authority). He (or it) is effective if there is an end for which he is an authority or for which the authority is exercised, and if that end is achieved in an appropriate manner; he (or it) is not effective if there is such an end but either it is not achieved or not achieved in an appropriate manner.

We have called the source of authority the basis upon which justification rests. We can call the person who exercises authority or who is an authority the bearer of authority. I shall refer to those over whom authority is exercised or those for whom someone else is an authority as the subjects of authority. The bearer of authority exercises or wields his authority in certain ways, and these can be called the means or instruments of the exercise of his authority. The actions or reactions of the subjects of authority can be called their "authority response." Thus we would expect one kind of authority response to an ineffective authority and a different response to an effective one. Hence, effectiveness and ineffectiveness can be described in terms of authority responses. Authority in general might be justified but certain kinds of authority found to be illegitimate; and authority might be both justified and legitimate though some particular exercise of it or some of the means of its exercise found to be illegitimate. Many kinds of "misfires" are possible.

We can further distinguish between the extent and intensity of authority. The extent of a person's authority is a function of the number of persons for whom he is an authority. A parent may be an authority for his child; a professor for his class; a President for his country. The extent of the authority of the professor is usually greater than of the parent and less than of the President. Intensity refers to the degree of acceptance of the authority by the subject of authority. If the authority of someone were, in a given case, a function of his knowledge, and if his being an authority involved his assertions being believed, a parent's authority would be more intense than a professor's — if the children of the former believed firmly what was said to them by the parent just because he said it, while the professor's students were inclined to believe what he said, but not very firmly. If authority involves obedience, then intensity might be a function of whether the subjects obeyed quickly and eagerly or with reluctance or only when there was also a threat of force.

The scope or range of a person's authority refers to the realms or fields in which he is an authority, or over which he exercises authority. A President might exercise a greater range of authority or his authority can be said to have greater scope than the authority exercised by a policeman. A very learned man might be an authority in several branches of learning and so the scope of his authority would be greater than that of someone who was an authority in only one of those branches. The authority of someone who was an authority in only one branch of knowledge might be deeper and more acute than that of someone else; in which case his authority would be better grounded.

The scope or range of authority is generally limited. If it is or is considered unlimited, then the bearer of such authority might be said to be a universal authority or to exercise universal authority.

I have mentioned that there are systems of authority. These systems establish certain structures; those specify who (or which positions) will be bearers of authority, the field and scope of that authority, and the instruments of its exercise; similarly they designate who will be the subjects of authority, and the proper authority response. A person may belong to a number of systems of authority and be a bearer of authority in one, a subject in another. He may find that there is a clash between what several authorities in different systems command. Within any field an authority is ultimate if there is no authority higher than it. Thus, to the extent that each state considers itself sovereign, a national government holds its authority ultimate in the field of law. Authority is absolute if there is none higher than it, and in any clash of authorities, or in any clash of authority with anything else, it reigns supreme and is to be obeyed. Whether there is any such thing as absolute authority, of course, remains open at this stage. Within some systems of authority, as is well known, authority may be delegated.

We have spoken of the bearer of authority as if he were a person. We should also leave open the possibility that the bearer of authority might be more than one person, and so we should not preclude speaking of collective authority or shared authority. Moreover, the bearer of authority might be a book, or as we saw in an early example of the way the word is used, it might be the law of a country, the rules of a game, or a tradition (tradition might be both the bearer of authority and, in a different sense, it is claimed by some to be a source of authority[1]).

Authority, considered as a right, or power, or quality, rather than as the person having authority, should be distinguished from and appropriately related to the concepts of power, right, and influence. Authority can be considered, in some of its forms, as a power or a kind of power. We speak of Congress having the power or authority to declare war. But, meaning the same thing, we also speak of Congress having the right or authority to declare war. Where the words are interchangeable, nothing hangs on whether we call authority a power or right. But there are other cases in which the words are *not* interchangeable. In certain instances we will also want to say that someone has the authority to do something but that he cannot back up his authority. It is empty, ineffective, powerless. Thus, though some kinds of authority are types of power, not all of them are. Similarly, though some types of authority are the same as right (for instance, a title to do certain acts), not all instances of it are. The case is similar with influence. When a President puts his influence behind something, it is sometimes appropriate to say he puts his authority behind it. But again, not all instances of authority are the same as exercising influence. Kurt Baier[2] distinguishes authority, influence and power by saying that power is necessarily grounded, influence is necessarily effective, and authority is not necessarily either. As he uses the terms the distinctions are correct. But they are insufficient; for if authority is grounded it is not necessarily the same as power; if it is effective it is not necessarily the same as influence; and it is certainly not the case that it is only authority when it is neither grounded nor effective. Baier, of course, does not claim that it is. But when we have made the distinctions he makes exactly what we have gained is not entirely clear. Some authority is an exercise of power; some is an exercise of influence; some is an exercise of a right to perform certain actions. But each of these in the abstract is not very enlightening. Part of the difficulty is that preciseness cannot be introduced until we find out what kinds of authority there are. For to act as if all kinds of authority were the same, as if they all had the same relation to power or right or influence, to force or coercion, would be to presume much of what has yet to be discussed and displayed. It may be the case that authority is greatest when least force is required, and that the less the authority, the greater the need for force and coercion. But this presupposes that all authority involves getting people to act in certain ways, that it is related to commands or obedience, which is not necessarily the case. For instance, when we looked initially at the uses of the word *authority*, we saw that we refer to some people as authorities in a certain field or discipline because of their knowledge. Such a person can be called *an epistemic authority*. But such an authority has no right or power to command simply because of his knowledge.[3] If he has such power it comes from his position or from some source other than his knowledge.

Some kinds of authority, however, do involve the right or power to command and these can be called types of executive authority. We can characterize executive authority as the right or power of X to do some action *a* with respect to field *b* in virtue of *c*.

At this stage of the discussion to call authority a right or a power is to purposely leave it ambiguous. From our previous examples we see that it is sometimes called one, sometimes called the other, and that in many cases ordinary language does not sharply distinguish between them. Sometimes one may have a right to do something but not in fact be able to do it; X may in this case be said to have the authority to do *a*, but his authority is ineffective. In the same sense one might be said to have the power to do *a* but be unable to do it, as when a government which has the power to raise taxes (meaning thereby the right to do so) is not able to collect any. In another sense, the power to do something implies the ability to do it; and right carries with it in some cases at least the added notion of prima facie (at first view) legitimacy. Not every right is a power and not every case of having power to do something implies the right to do it. The notion of authority straddles both concepts; it is sometimes referred to as a right, sometimes as a power, sometimes as both together, and sometimes ambiguously as either of them. We can capture some of the nuances by employing the distinctions we developed earlier, viz.

legitimate and illegitimate, effective and ineffective, *de facto* and *de jure*, formal and informal. Not every instance of a right or of a power is an instance of authority, though in every instance of executive authority there is at least some claim being made about a right or a power.

It should also be clear that to speak of authority as a power in no way involves the notion of force or coercion. When we say that a justice of the peace has the power to perform a marriage cere- mony, we are speaking of his legal ability to do so; we are not granting him, or recognizing in him, any right to use force or coercion. The appropriate sense of power here is 'ability'. When the United States Constitution lists the "powers of Congress" it lists those things which it is authorized by the Constitution to do, or those things that it and it alone has the right to do under the Constitution. The right to use force might be a right or a power given to certain people, for example, to the police in the fulfill- ment of their obligations. But authority itself does not necessarily involve force or coercion.

The right or power at issue in executive authority is always the right or power to perform some action. In this way it is distin- guished from epistemic authority. There are two broad categories of such actions which we can call imperative and performatory. The first involves X's commanding or ordering some subject Y to perform a certain action. The second involves X's doing some- thing other than issuing a command, such as acting as an author- ized agent for a group (as a Treasurer paying bills for an Association), or as the bearer of a particular type of power, for example, being empowered to perform a marriage ceremony. In both of the latter cases X performs some act in virtue of some specific right or power granted or delegated to him.

The field *b* to which his authority is restricted depends on the kind of authority he has, the source of that authority, the position he occupies, the circumstances, and similar considerations. The range of the authority of a justice of the peace is more limited than that of the Governor of California, though the latter might have no right to do some of the things the former is authorized to do. Executive authority, in the sense I am using it here, encompasses what is frequently referred to as executive, judicial, and legislative authority. A totalitarian government might claim unlimited authority, and so might claim that in some sense its field is unlimited. Obviously, in the vast majority of cases the scope of authority either claimed, recognized or justifiable is limited.

To specify that it is in virtue of c that X has the right or power to do a is to tie the notion of executive authority to a system or context. C might be a set of laws, or a constitution, or a tradition, or a position, or a set of personal qualities appropriate to a set of circumstances. They form the context in which authority operates, and they are essential to an understanding of executive authority. Executive authority cannot be understood in abstraction from a context, for it is defined by the context. Why people either do or should obey commands or allow others to act for them or accept an individual's signature as binding a group, and so on, can be made intelligible only in terms of given contexts. A justice of the peace has the right to perform a marriage ceremony within a framework of civil law; a business executive has the right to tell his secretary to take a letter in virtue of the structure of the business, their respective roles, and some agreement as to work and pay.

Since we have characterized executive authority as the right or power of X to do a in b in virtue of c, we have restricted X to being an agent, usually a person. When we speak of law or rules of a game as authorities, or when we speak of the authority of law or rules, we are *not* speaking of them as executive authorities or as if they had executive authority, though they may be the source of such authority.

De facto executive authority is the weakest sense of executive authority. By starting with it we can describe and discuss the phenomenon of executive authority, whether or not such authority is ever legitimate.

We can characterize *de facto* imperative executive authority by specifying the action of X within the above definition as being one of issuing a command, and by describing the response of the recipient of the command, Y. X is a *de facto* imperative executive authority if, when he issues some command q to Y, Y performs q because it was commanded by X; q being something in field b and in a context c which is legitimate, *de jure,* or which Y accepts as legitimate or *de jure* (whether or not it is).

Now the strength of the word 'command' may vary, and there are various ways to issue a command, some more formal and some less so. The command may be stated politely as a request or as a wish, but in the context it is understood by Y as being equivalent to a command or order. The command of an executive authority should be distinguished on the one hand from a command in a context of force or violence, where X commands Y to do *q* under some immediate coercive threat. The command of a gunman to a bank teller to hand over her cash drawer would not be a case of imperative authority even if the teller obeyed the command. Nor would it be a case of executive authority if Y, a friend of X's, did *q*, which X had strongly requested, simply because Y wished to help his friend in the way requested. Y's motive in doing *q* is sometimes important; hence the necessity of the stipulation that *q* be within field *b*, in a context governing that field, and of defining the relation of X and Y, such that the command is legitimate or *de jure* within the system or that Y feels the command is legitimate as a command. To be a *de facto* authority is a function either of system or of acceptance.

Motives are frequently complex. Fear might be part of the reason for Y's doing *q* — for example, fear of losing one's job, or fear of being court martialed — just as love, or affection, or a desire to please, or the hope of receiving special treatment, or a raise or a promotion might be part of the motive for doing *q*. Y might even anticipate what X will command and save him the trouble of commanding it by doing it before commanded. Empirically, therefore, and in the absence of institutionalized structures, it frequently may be difficult to decide whether a given action by Y constitutes X as a *de facto* authority. The intensity of X's authority in such instances is a function of Y's acceptance of him as an authority, and the intensity may vary from almost none to complete acceptance.

Performatory authority is more difficult to circumscribe because it can encompass such a multitude of different kinds of actions. In general X has *de facto* performatory executive authority if in virtue of his occupying some position within a system or context he is given the right or power to perform some action *a*,

or he is believed by Y to have the right or power to do so. Someone
can be made a *de facto* executive authority, therefore, either by
occupying a certain position which carries with it certain rights
or powers, or by being accorded certain rights and powers implicitly by those who accept his actions in these spheres as legitimate,
even though he does not actually occupy the office which would
entitle him to those rights or powers. In the first case he may hold
the proper office but his actions may not be accepted, in which
case his authority is ineffective. In the second case he may be a
pretender to the throne or an impersonator or a fraud, and yet the
acceptance of his actions by others constitutes the acceptance
behavior necessary to make him a *de facto* authority, though an
illegitimate one. An alternative way to describe the latter case
would be to say that X has no authority, and that though the
compliance behavior on the part of Y is such that it would be
appropriate if X did have the authority Y thinks he does, X does
not and cannot attain authority in this way. This would be to
restrict the use of the word *authority* to legitimate authority. The
reason, once again, for preferring to classify cases of illegitimate
authority as cases of authority is that it becomes possible to describe such cases as perceived and to handle them even if there is
no such thing as legitimate authority.

Now there are a variety of contexts in which we find executive
authority, and of these we can specify at least three general types.
One of these is the family or the natural society; a second is the
state or civil society; and a third is a free contractual-type organization or society. The first is the social unit into which one is
born, and it yields a natural relation which exists between parents
and children. The executive authority of the parents can be called
parental (or in an earlier period, paternalistic) authority. A child
is usually born into a civil society as well, and most people have
no choice but to belong to some such society or other, though they
may in some instances leave a certain country and join the civil
society in some other country. The kind of executive authority
appropriate to civil society I shall call imperial authority. There
are, in addition to the family and civil society, a great many organizations, clubs, societies, corporations, and the like which one
might join, each of which is governed by certain rules. It may also

be the case that some group is formed spontaneously with someone exercising leadership without there being any formal rules. In either case the authority is authority within a free association of some sort, and I shall term such authority operative authority. The three kinds of authority may overlap in certain instances and they may also be found mixed with other kinds of authority.

There are also ambiguous cases. Suppose someone is ill and he goes to his doctor who tells him, "Take one of these pills three times a day for the next week, and then come back and see me." Is this an instance of executive imperative authority?

The ambiguity comes from the fact that there is no organization or established set of rules making the doctor an executive authority empowered to command his patients in the area of health. The patient-doctor relationship is an informal one in which it is expected that both doctor and patient are interested in the patient's health, and that the patient goes to the doctor for advice and instruction. The doctor is an epistemic authority, and we have seen that epistemic authority entails no right to command. What the doctor does when he tells the patient to take certain pills can be interpreted as a shortened form of a hypothetical imperative. He is in fact saying, "If you want to feel better, or if you want to cure whatever it is you have, then take these pills." Since he assumes that the patient is interested in feeling better and in curing his sickness (otherwise he would not have come to the doctor), he suppresses the first part of the above statement, and simply gives the last part of the imperative. The patient knows that the doctor has no right to command him or to force him to follow his advice, though the patient ignores such advice at his own peril or discomfort. If someone feels that his doctor is incompetent or his advice poor, he is free to go to another doctor or to ignore the doctor's advice or prescription. The right of a patient not to be operated on without his consent, for instance, is usually protected in the United States by law. Now despite all this, patients frequently react the same way to the imperatives or prescriptions of a doctor as they do to someone who holds executive imperative authority; and in these cases we can say that the doctor is a *de facto* executive authority with respect to such patients.

The justification for his exercising such authority is the fact that he has at heart the same end that his patient has, namely the cure of his patient's ills, and by his commanding him to act in certain ways he helps his patient attain what the patient himself desires. The fact is, however, that a doctor has no right to force a patient to follow his advice, though he may threaten him with the natural consequences which will probably follow if the doctor is correct and the patient does not do as he is told. Neither formal structure nor the doctor's knowledge nor the good of the patient are sufficient for the doctor to attempt to force the patient to obey. The doctor is not a *de jure* executive authority for his patient (the case might be different in the army, but then the doctor's right or power to command stems from his rank, not from his profession). If the doctor is a *de facto* executive authority for his patients, he is such because his patients make him such. But he has no right to demand that they treat him as such an authority, and no strict right to command them. Hence, strictly speaking, the executive authority which he enjoys and wields over his patients is, in the sense that it is not a right, illegitimate. His legitimate function is to issue hypothetical imperatives, to make his knowledge available and to use his skill when it is desired by those on whom he uses it. The question of the authority he has in a hospital with respect to the other staff of that hospital, is of course, an entirely different matter, and in that context he may, by virtue of the rules of the hospital, enjoy a different kind of executive imperative authority, which is legitimate in terms of the rules, and which may well be *de jure*. In this case his authority is operative authority.

The doctor's orders can be considered as completely compatible with the patient's autonomy. For what the patient wills is not whatever the doctor orders, but his own health. His decision to act as the doctor prescribes is simply a decision to take the means appropriate to achieve his end. No obedience, therefore, is owed to the doctor, as is clear when the patient pays the doctor for his services or advice. The doctor who orders a heart patient to stop smoking has no way of enforcing that order and no right to enforce it if his patient is a mature, competent, outpatient. The doctor has no right to coerce such a patient into acting in certain ways, even for the good of the patient, though he may certainly reason with him and try to convince him to act as is best for him.

Some of a doctor's activities are covered by law, and by law he is given the authority to do certain things, such as prescribe drugs, thereby making available to a patient what would not be available to him without a prescription. Such authority is obviously not any authority he has merely because of his certification, perhaps because of his licensing, all of which, in most contemporary countries, are governed by law.

The authority of a lawyer is in some ways similar to that of a doctor. His client may go to him for advice, and take advantage of his knowledge, with no obligation to follow that advice, which he usually pays for. A client may also authorize his lawyer to represent him in a court or elsewhere, just as he might authorize his doctor to operate on him. The patient or client can authorize others to act on or for him. This might be called a kind of permissive delegated authority, for it does not constitute a command to the doctor to operate or to the lawyer to plead a case. The doctor and the lawyer receive one kind of performatory authority from the law, i.e. they are given the right to operate and to plead in court by the laws and rules governing such activities. This authority is contingent if the laws and rules require the permission of the patient or client who are thereby authorized to authorize the doctor and lawyer in turn. The client both authorizes the lawyer to represent him, and then usually pays him to do so.

Implicit in both the cases of the patient's or the client's authorization of the doctor and of the lawyer is the right of the individual to lead his own life, secure from certain kinds of interference. This can be expressed by saying he has the authority to lead his own life, to authorize others to do certain things to him (though there may well be limits; for example, he may not have the right to authorize someone to kill him) and for him. This might be said to be a kind of imperative authority, where the imperatives are self-given, and the limits to such authority may be the limits imposed by morality.[4] But as in the case of the doctor's authority and the lawyer's, there is some ambiguity in how exactly or even how best to classify this type of authority.

Now it should be clear that the types of authority which I have thus far tentatively identified are not mutually exclusive in that the same office and the same person may exercise several different types of authority. Someone may exercise parental authority over his children in virtue of his position, biological relationship, and their need, and he may also have authority over them which is sanctioned by law. A leader of a state may have duly constituted imperial authority and be an epistemic authority as well, and so on.

We have not examined whether executive authority of any type can be justified, and if so, how. If a general justification for the various types can be developed, we will then need the kinds of individual justifications, together with possible principles of limitation, which may be appropriate and valid. If there can be found adequate grounds and justifications for authority, we should further inquire whether the exercise of authority is ever properly absolute, and if not, which principles can be established for its limitation. We should also inquire whether, in case of conflict, we can determine any a priori ranking of the types of authority, and which holds precedence in case of conflict.

Even from the little that has been said thus far, it should be obvious that authority is never found in isolation and by itself. It always forms part of a social fabric and setting. How the various kinds operate within the varied social settings will depend, in part, on their purported function and supposed justification. But it also will depend partly on the institutions themselves. An analysis of the concept of authority can take us only so far; but only if the concept is clear can principles of justification and of limitation of authority — including that authority which involves power — be found.

NOTES

1. Carl J. Friedrich, *Tradition and Authority* (London, Macmillan, 1972).
2. Kurt Baier, The justification of governmental authority. *The Journal of Philosophy* LXIX: 702-710, 1972.
3. Richard T. De George, The nature and function of epistemic authority. In R. Baine Harris, (ed.) *Authority: A Philosophical Analysis*. (University of Alabama, University of Alabama Press, 1976).

4. Richard T. De George, Authority and morality. In F. J. Adelmann, (ed.), *Authority* (The Hague, Martinus Nijhoff, 1974): pp. 31-49.

5

CONTROLLING: THE USE OF
AUTHORITY, POWER, AND INFLUENCE*

PAUL WHISENAND and R. FRED FERGUSON

ONE of the most exciting and complicated products invented by mankind thus far is the magnificent jet airliner, a unique blend of materials and systems brought together for a specific purpose. Perhaps not so exciting, but nonetheless complicated, is the modern police organization, a unique blend of personalities brought together in a most complicated society for a specific purpose. Regardless of the beauty or ability of the wondrous jet aircraft, its continued operation would be impossible without control. Greater control provides for greater reliability in reaching all its stated goals. The same holds true for any organization, but perhaps none more critically so than the modern police organization. Obviously the jet aircraft can operate — for a time at least — with some rather loosely handled controls. But in the end poor control is the harbinger of failure. The same is true of the modern police organization.

Perhaps the greatest difference in the analogy is that aircraft failure is normally consummated in one obvious and final plunge. On the other hand, a police organization without proper control may struggle along for some time, with few outward signs of crises. The inward signs are, of course, more apparent — absenteeism, employee turnover, inefficiency, apathy toward the public served, and perhaps the most damaging of all in terms of the total police service, dishonesty and general corruption.

We are not suggesting that every policing agency should have controls of the same magnitude. Obviously a two-man police department is not likely to have the same communication problems as will a department of five or five hundred men and women.

---

*Paul M. Whisenand and R. Fred Ferguson, *The Managing of Police Organizations*, ©1973. Reprinted by permission of Prentice-Hall, Inc., Englewood Cliffs, New Jersey.

As police organizations grow in size, it is proportionately less likely that every member will have a clear understanding and acceptance of organizational goals. More controls will undoubtedly be necessary to insure reasonable goal achievement.

The President's Commission on Law Enforcement and Administration of Justice displayed substantial concern for the internal control of police agencies in its 1967 *Task Force Report: The Police.* Its observations and recommendations are especially relevant to this chapter. The report clearly states the critical need for adequate control. It also defines the methods by which controls or their lack prevent the organization from reaching broader expectations and goals. The following section is drawn from this report.

Internal Controls

It is in the nature of an administrative organization that the establishment of policies to guide the exercise of discretion by individuals is not enough. There is need also for the development of methods for assuring compliance. This requires a system of administrative controls to be applied within an agency.

Methods of Internal Control

An analysis of patterns of deviations from appropriate policy standards indicates that such deviations usually fall into three general categories: situations in which an officer violates departmental regulations or policies; situations in which an officer's behavior is considered improper, but does not constitute a violation of existing department policy; and situations in which an officer's behavior is clearly illegal or improper, but is consistent with the routine practice of the particular agency and is generally condoned by its administration.

1. There are a limited number of situations today in which police administrators have issued policy statements to control police conduct. These tend to mirror the requirements of appellate cases as, for example, policies to implement the specific interrogation requirements of the *Miranda* case. Field studies conducted by the commission indicate that such policies,

promulgated at the top of the agency, are often disregarded in practice. Occasionally situations may arise in which a failure to adhere to existing policy becomes a source of embarrassment to the top echelons of the police agency, as, for example, if a failure to give the warnings required by the *Miranda* case were to prevent the conviction of a dangerous criminal in a highly publicized case.

The fact that administrative policy for dealing with crime or potential crime situations does not have a very significant impact upon the actions of individual officers appears to be primarily attributable to two factors: the ambivalent attitude which often accompanies the pronouncement of a policy implementing a decision like *Miranda,* and competing influences brought to bear by subordinate command staff who are subject to more immediate pressures from the community they serve.

Top police officials have been quite outspoken in registering their opposition to recent decisions of the U. S. Supreme Court. Personnel within an agency are fully aware of the public pronouncements of their superiors. They recognize that an order which purports to urge compliance with a recent decision is necessitated by the decision and is reluctantly issued by their superiors. Without a special effort on the part of the administrator to distinguish between his right to enter into public debate over the wisdom of court decisions and the need for compliance with court decisions, it is likely that departmental policies which simply mirror the requirements of an appellate decision will be largely disregarded.

A somewhat similar situation exists when operating personnel believe that a change in departmental policy reflects a somewhat reluctant effort on the part of the administration to appease some community group that has made a complaint against the department.

In current practice, such departmental policy as exists is but one of a number of competing considerations that influence police actions at the operating level. Tremendous pressures are generated upon the various command levels in a large police agency by community groups — pressures from which such personnel cannot be easily isolated. The desire on the part of a supervisory officer or precinct commander to satisfy a prominent citizen, to meet the demands of a community group on whose support his continued effectiveness and acceptance depend, to obtain favorable publicity, or simply to satisfy his most immediate superior, may override any desire he may have to adhere to established policy. Subordinates, in turn, have their eyes upon their superior rather than upon formal pronouncements which come to them in written form. The extent to which they conform with policy formulated at the top levels will be determined, in large measure, by the spirit and tone in which it is communicated to them by their more immediate superiors. Each of the many levels of supervision in a large agency, therefore, constitutes a point at which policies may be diluted or ignored.

2. An entirely different set of problems is raised when an individual officer acts in a manner which none of his superiors would condone, but there is no formulated policy to serve as a basis for discipline or condemnation.

The problems are complicated by the peculiar nature of the police function. Officers are usually spread out about an entire city. They do not have the opportunity for immediate consultation with superior officers when called upon to take action. The danger of mass disorder is always present, and the need for quick decisions often requires that the officer take some form of action before he has the opportunity to acquire all of the facts. It is, therefore, difficult for the police administrator to hold an individual police officer to the same standard one would hold a person who had an opportunity to consult and to think about the matter before acting.

The actions of individual police officers are not easily subject to review. Contacts between police officers and citizens are often contentious, tending to evoke an emotional response on the part of both the officer and the citizen. They occur at times and in locations where others are not present. And an informal code among police officers, which bands individual officers together for mutual support when challenged from the outside, silences fellow police officers who may be the only witnesses to an incident. As a consequence the typical complaint will consist of an assertion of wrongdoing on the part of a citizen and a denial by the officer. There usually is no available basis for corroborating either story. The consequence of continually disbelieving the officer would obviously mean a loss of morale. Hence, the tendency in such cases is for the police administrator to accept the officer's version unless there is some reason to believe the officer is being untruthful.

3. The most complicated situations that arise in current practice are those in which the actions of an officer are clearly illegal or improper but are consistent with prevailing practices of a department. Such practices are commonly found in the police agencies serving large urban areas, where the practices constitute part of the informal response which the police have developed for dealing with problems of a recurring nature. It is, for example, common for police officers to search the interior of a vehicle without legal grounds in high crime-rate areas. It is similarly common for police to search gamblers or arrest known prostitutes without adequate grounds. Since such actions are generally encouraged by superior officers, it is inconceivable that the officer would be administratively criticized or disciplined upon the filing of a complaint. Nevertheless, complaints tend to be processed administratively in the same way as complaints alleging a violation of administrative policy by an officer. As a consequence, the complaint procedure does not serve as a vehicle to challenge and cause a reconsideration of policies which are sanctioned by the department even though not articulated.

Proposed Improvements in Methods of Internal Control

Some of the problems of achieving control over the conduct of individual police officers would be simplified if there were a commitment by the police administrator to a systematic policy-formulation process. This would require specific attention to present unarticulated policies which are clearly illegal and as a consequence would create administrative pressure to reject them or develop alternatives rather than assume the indefensible position of formally adopting illegal practices as official departmental policy. The development of adequate policy statements would afford the individual police officers greater guidance with respect to important decisions like the use of force, and the decision to arrest or to search.

But the mere adoption of administrative policies will not alone achieve compliance. This will require "good administration," that is, the use of the whole array of devices commonly employed in public administration to achieve conformity. These include, but are not limited to, the setting of individual responsibility, the establishment of systems of accountability, the designing of procedures for checking and reporting on performance, and the establishment of methods for taking corrective action.

The police administrator currently achieves a high degree of conformity on the part of officers to standards governing such matters as the form of dress, the method of completing reports, and the procedures for processing of citizen complaints. Sleeping on duty, leaving one's place of assignment without authorization, or failing to meet one's financial obligations are all situations against which supervisory personnel currently take effective action.

The success of internal controls as applied to such matters appears to be dependent upon two major factors: (1) the attitude and commitment of the head of the agency to the policies being enforced and (2) the degree to which individual officers and especially supervisory officers have a desire to conform.

The average police administrator, for example, has no ambivalence over accepting responsibility for the physical appearance of his men. He does not wait to act until complaints are received from a third party. He undertakes, instead, by a variety of administrative techniques, to produce a desire in his subordinates to conform. This desire may reflect an agreement by the subordinates with the policy. Or it may reflect respect for their superior, a lack of interest one way or the other, or a fear of punishment or reprisal. Whatever the reason, the officer in a sort of "state of command" does what he is told rather than follow a course of his own choosing.

In sharp contrast, the police administrator is typically ambivalent over the responsibility he has for controlling the activities of his force in the exercise of discretionary power in dealing with crime or potential crime situations. While he views the physical appearance of his men as his concern, he often sees the methods by which the law is enforced as involving matters which are the primary responsibility of others outside the police establishment. This deference may, in part, be attributable to the sharing of responsibilities with other agencies — particularly the courts. Unlike internal matters over which the police administrator has complete control, much of what the police do relating to crime and criminals is dependent for approval upon the decisions of nonpolice agencies.

Strengthening of administrative control requires the creation of the same sense of personal responsibility on the part of the police administrator for the implementation of proper law enforcement policies as he presently has for implementing policies relating to internal matters.

This will require that the administrator be given the education, training, and resources necessary to fulfill the role. It requires also a change in what is expected of police administrators by the public and by those occupying key positions in other agencies in the criminal justice system. Police officials cannot be expected to develop a sense of responsibility, if they are treated like ministerial officers, and excluded from important policy-making decisions, such as those regarding the revision of substantive and procedural laws.

Also required is the development of a professional identification which can serve police officers as a frame of reference within which they can see the importance of their conforming to appropriate law enforcement policies. Blind obedience to orders, such as is currently elicited for some aspects of police operations, is limited in both its values and desirability to purely administrative functions. Personnel called upon to deal with complex problems of human behavior and expected to make decisions on the basis of professionally developed criteria must, themselves, have some form of professional identification as a common basis from which to function.

Professional identification has, for example, been a major element in the rapid development of what are now some of our more highly regarded correctional systems. With training and education in social casework as a prerequisite to employment, operating personnel function from a framework for decision-making which is consistent with and supportive of departmental policies. The whole administrative process is facilitated because both administrators and field personnel are on the same "wave length," talking the same language and supporting the same values.

A somewhat similar development is essential in the police field. Individual police officers must be provided with the training and education which will give them a professional identification consistent with the police role in a free society. Such training and education will equip them to understand the policies of their superiors, make them receptive to efforts to make law enforcement both fair and effective, and enable the officer to take appropriate action in the unpredictable situations not dealt with by even the best efforts at policy formulation.[1]

Private Organizations

Private business organizations have consistently moved ahead of government in recognizing the need and in searching for greater efficiency control. This is not to say that government and, more specifically, policing organizations have not exercised controls, for they have. But apparently there has been and continues to be a primary reliance, almost a preoccupation by many, upon hierarchical authority. We are not suggesting that traditional concepts of authority, responsibility, and accountability be scrapped or bypassed. We are suggesting that the state of the managerial art has progressed to the point that it offers other options and complementing additions.

In recognizing the necessity for more effective controls, private organizations have had at least one built-in motivating factor not shared by government — profit. Private organizations simply cannot continue to exist without profit. On the other hand, we believe that police organizations in the future will be asked to operate at a profit; that is, profit in terms of greater, more efficient services for the people served. Traditionally, police organizations have grown proportionately with the general population. As police goals and expectations have expanded, the growth has become somewhat disproportional. Our belief is that police organizations will not be able to solve tomorrow's problems by simply adding new personnel, nor will there be the dollars to do so. Perhaps, then, it is reasonable to look to business for some of the answers. Granted, there are vast differences between government and private business; however, one theme that we trust will emerge in the following chapters is that the similarities are greater than these differences. If we, the writers and the reader, can agree with this idea, then perhaps we can also agree that many managerial concepts and rules held to be truths by business managers and contemporary writers in that field are applicable to the modern police organization.

George D. Eastman, professor and director of the Institute of Government Research and Services at Kent State University, as editor of *Municipal Police Administration* gave some recognition to this same proposition in his discussion of the principles of organization:

> Students of public and police administration, sooner or later in the course of their studies, are presented with "principles of organization." The principles often are offered as organization dogma and their acceptance taken for granted. Thoughtful people in business, industry, and government, however, have long since questioned their validity. General merit of the so-called principles is not basically at issue; rather, there is a challenge to their universality of application. It would seem appropriate, at this time, to simply identify them as a set of concepts or propositions believed by many to be a basis for sound organization.
>
> Confusion exists in their presentation because some relate to structure and some to process; in the sense of process some could be considered more meaningfully as matters of administrative action. Nonetheless, an organization structure should assure reasonably that there is provision for:
> 1. Sound and clear-cut allocation of responsibilities;
> 2. Equitable distribution of work loads among elements and individuals;
> 3. Clear and unequivocal lines of authority;
> 4. Authority adequate to discharge assigned responsibilities;
> 5. Reasonable spans of control for administrative, command, and supervisory officers;
> 6. Unity of command;

7. Coordination of effort;
8. Administrative control.

Significantly the organization can only "make provision for" but cannot guarantee anything. It has no life or vitality of its own; it is simply a vehicle for management. As Urwick says, "It is the men and not the organization chart that do the work."[2]

Formalization and Authority

As in police organizations, private organizations tend to formalize their hierarchical structure in the pyramidal shape. Pyramids are convenient in that they clearly signify differences in rank; the higher one's position in the pyramid, the greater one's responsibility and authority. Perhaps private organizations have fewer levels of responsibility within the pyramid, nonetheless there exists the theory of increasing responsibility and authority while conversely the span of control is diminished. The pyramid permits a centralized control over the organization and places the final responsibility and authority in the hands of a single individual.

Authority

It becomes clear, then, that authority resides in the position. Superiors in any organization tend to rely on their rank authority to resolve organizational conflict, to change behavior — the superior being identified as the changer, the subordinate the changee. The use of authority to bring about change in behavior is expeditious, to say the least. Unfortunately, authority does not necessarily guarantee the degree or permanence of change.

Organizational heads are commonly held responsible for the formalization of policy that will assist the organization toward its stated goals. In police organizations, authority to bring about desired change is commonly exhibited in the form of general orders and departmental manuals. The following example is extracted from the *Manual of the Los Angeles Police Department*:

4/292. **Disposing of rewards and gratuities.** When an employee receives a reward or contribution, he shall transmit it to the

Commander, Personnel and Training Bureau, for deposit in the
Fire and Police Pension Fund.

If an employee is given a check or money order coming within
the meaning of this Section, he shall endorse it "Pay to the
Order of the City of Los Angeles," followed by his signature as it
appears on the face. In addition, he shall complete two copies of
the Employee's Report, Form 15.7, which shall be transmitted
with the reward or contribution to the Personnel and Training
Bureau and shall include the following information:
° Name and address of person giving the reward or contribution.
° Reason for giving reward or contribution.
° Amount of the reward or contribution.[3]

Responsibility with commensurate authority to insure that the
regulation is carried out is delegated to subordinates down to the
appropriate level. In our opinion, however, it is pure fallacy to
assume that the implied authority of the written order has any
greater degree of success than that of the spoken word.

Harold J. Leavitt, in his book *Managerial Psychology,* has
depicted interesting pros and cons of the use of authority:

> From the manager's viewpoint the advantages of authority,
> especially restrictively used authority, are huge. We have al-
> ready cited one of them, the control and coordination advan-
> tage. There are many others, too.
>
> For one thing, one doesn't have to know much about any
> particular Joe Doaks to be fairly certain that firing him or cut-
> ting his pay or demoting him will strike at some important
> needs and thereby keep him in line. But one might have to know
> a good deal about the same employee to find out how to make
> work more fun for him.
>
> A corollary advantage, then, is simplicity. Authority as a
> restrictive tool does not require much subtlety or much under-
> standing of people's motives. How simple it is to spank a child
> when he misbehaves, and how difficult and complicated to
> distract him or provide substitute satisfactions or to "explain"
> the situation. Given a hundred children, how much easier it is
> to keep them in line by punishing a few recalcitrants than to
> teach them all to feel "responsible." ...
>
> Restrictive authority has another kind of advantage: speed. A
> do-it-or-else order eliminates the time consuming dillydallying
> of feedback. ...

Employees who expect to be censured whenever they are caught loafing may learn to *act* busy (and *when* to act busy) and also that the boss is an enemy. They are thereby provided with a challenging game to play against the boss: who can think up the best ways of loafing without getting caught; a game in which they can feel that justice is on their side and a game they can usually win. . . .

The tenuousness and the self-defeating weakness of reliance on restrictive authority becomes apparent right here. When his authority has been "undermined" by the "sabotage" of subordinates, the superior who has depended on authority is likely immediately to assume that what he needs is *more authority,* because authority is the only tool he knows how to use.[4]

Power

Although some of Leavitt's examples may appear rather simplistic or basic, his message that authority is an important element of organizational control, of change, is quite clear. On the other hand, Leavitt is just as resolute that reliance upon pure authority leaves the superior with very little reason for security.[5]

In discussing the concept of authority, social scientists Pfiffner and Sherwood observe that authority implies the *right* to command another person, and the subordinate person has the *duty* to obey the command. They make specific note, however, that "the *right* to command does not necessarily connote the *capacity* to command."[6]

Since most law enforcement agencies are developed around the military model, authority in this case does afford a superior the ability to exercise, to a lesser or greater extent depending upon his hierarchical level, control over the subordinate's continued employment, salary increases (merit principle), work hours, assignments, promotions, and infinite other rewards and punishments. The superior does not, however, own the subordinate, nor can he hope for much more than a rather limited control. It is the subordinate, in the end, who makes the decision of whether or not it is worth it; in fact, whether or not he should report for work at all. Authority in a police organization, then, has its limitations.

Power, on the other hand, resides in the person, not necessarily in the position. It may or may not coincide with the official structure of authority. Power in itself is not institutionalized in the sense that one can look to the organizational manual and find out where it resides.[7] Conversely, almost every organization or organizational unit has the "person to see." Typical of such persons is the boss's secretary, the boss's assistant, the boss's wife. Other people, of course, may hold this same power potential, though remaining less obvious. It is not unusual for persons to be totally unaware of their own power potential. This normally occurs where the power is deferred. This is to say that the influencing party may be operating at several levels removed from the point of action. Power, simply stated, is the ability to influence behavior.

While we have taken care to emphasize that true power does not necessarily follow hierarchical lines or authoritative positions, the advantage to authoritative figures who also possess concomitant power should be obvious.

The term *power,* perhaps because of its own ominous sound, sometimes connotes being deceitful, or even illegitimate. The reader should bear in mind, however, that the expert, the consultant, exhibits power; that the person whose opinion is respected exhibits power; and that often a person who is simply "liked," who for one reason or another is an attractive person, exhibits power.

Bennis more clearly describes power as falling into five components:

1. *Coercive power,* or the ability of A to reward and/or punish B;

2. *Referent, or identification power* or the influence which accrues to A because he (or the group) is attractive, a person whom B wants to like and be liked by — in short, a role model;

3. *Expert power,* or the power that we associate with science and "truth";

4. *Legitimate* or *traditional* power, or power which stems from institutional norms and practices and from historical-legal traditions;

5. *Value power,* or influence which is gained on the basis of attraction to the values of A.[8]

Pfiffner and Sherwood have defined power as the politics of how things get done.[9] Though not particularly profound, it is important to recognize that in the real political arena, authoritative heads, while occupying a position of relative importance, must rely a great deal upon their knowledge of where the power politics lies; otherwise they cannot hope to carry out long-range programs and goals. They can, of course, heroically buck the power, but heroics cannot be relied upon to "get things done." Internal power politics is a part of every organization and police departments are no exception; to deny its existence and to neglect its utilization is foolhardy.

Pfiffner and Sherwood's definition has special meaning when viewing *power* as a component of organization control. Obviously, if the *power* is held by persons other than those in authority, it becomes a matter of political necessity for the authority figures to have access to that power. This becomes especially sticky for the "old guard" type of police manager who simply is not accustomed to "dealing" with subordinates. When an administrator fails to recognize the realities of present-day organizational politics, the result is often a friction-building impasse that causes organizational dysfunction. As we stated earlier, authoritative failure usually results in a drive for more authority which, of course, further complicates the problem.

Practitioners in the field can no doubt conjure up their own nightmarish recollection of examples in which the administrator got himself so far out on a limb that it was finally chopped off. Administrative heads of government tend to back their police managers when the first internal conflicts arise, but history has shown that sooner or later their support wanes.

At this late point the police manager should recognize the political facts of life and change his style, utilizing the organizational power politics to its best advantage. In many cases where the unswerving managerial style prevails, however, the manager is eventually demoted, retired, fired, or elevated to a state of limbo where he no longer has any influence. There are, of course, those few who have acquired considerable personal power through outside-of-the-organization politics. They seem to remain almost indefinitely, surrounded by a kind of bureaucratic moat, blindly impeding the organization and its individual elements from reaching optimum goals.

We are in general agreement with contemporaries in the field that authority is an essential component of power, while power itself is not necessarily synonymous with authority. Power and authority are, however, legitimately a part of control.

Influence

In the following paragraphs we will be using the term *influence* in the most positive sense. Influence in our context then, as an element of control, means giving recognition and support to the hypotheses that people are more likely to do what is desired of them with minimum formal control — supervision — if they are *self-motivated*. To establish continuity with other contemporary writers in the field, the term *self-actualization* will be used synonymously with *self-motivation* throughout the discussion.

Influence, at least effective influence in modern organization, is not limited to a "top-down" system. Effective managers in the private sector have for some time realized that influence should flow in all directions, at all levels. Contemporary behavioral scientists generally agree that organizations in which subordinates as well as superiors feel a personal sense of influence are most likely to be highly productive. We believe this to be true of modern police organizations as well.

The police manager who has developed modern leadership skills, who has learned to consider the personal needs of his subordinates and has given them a feeling of self-importance, of worth, is likely to have a high-producing unit. *Feedback* is certainly not new to the police manager, but the kind of feedback in which the subordinate's opinion is respected, even solicited, and has direct influence on the organizational operations may well be. This type of subordinate influence, which at times may manifest itself in the form of criticism or at least appears to question the superior's judgment, can be quite threatening, especially if the manager has not gained a proper level of leadership sophistication. Actually, a substantial degree of personal security must always be present for all who participate in the use of influence for organizational effectiveness. This kind of security, together with satisfactory relationships between the manager and the managed, is the cohesiveness that builds effective organizations.

Through research, Rensis Likert in *New Patterns of Management* has verified that high-producing managers build better management systems than do low-producing managers. Likert discovered that a better management system, "while giving the men more influence, also gives the higher producing manager more influence."[10]

Likert's study did not reveal that all high-producing managers use the "influence" concept. Our own experience in police organizations offers some confirmation of this. Highly structured, highly authoritarian, highly bureaucratic, highly goal-centered police management systems can also be high producers. High production is used in this case to denote impressive statistics in the solution of crimes, the repression of traffic accidents, and all the other bench marks traditional with police agencies.

These data, however, do not reveal other important factors, such as employee attitudes, which present themselves in less-measurable ways — excessive absenteeism, employee turnover, negative discipline, and the like. High production, then, is not necessarily a barometer of organizational health and does not insure the internalization of organizational goals by the employee.

One can expect that subordinates in such a system will operate "by the book." They will tend not to extend themselves beyond what is considered to be their responsibility. Blau and Scott, in their study of formal organizations, were concerned with the results of routinized jobs of certain workers. They discovered that "the contractual bond of nonsupervisory white collar employees to formal organizations normally obligates them to fulfill role prescriptions only in accordance with minimum standards."[11]

To relate this to the police officer, he may be producing at a level acceptable to his supervisor, but if Blau and Scott's finding is applicable, he is normally only producing at an acceptable minimum; he has the capacity to do more with proper control — in this case motivation, self-actualization.

While statistics, or whatever measurement used to determine

organizational effectiveness, may appear encouraging, a careful examination must be made of the more vital signs of organizational health, such as employee morale, tardiness, absenteeism, turnover, and the growing necessity for negative disciplinary measures. If statistics is the game being played, subordinates soon learn to play the game, not unlike an earlier example of learning to "look busy" when the boss is around. True organizational health is more difficult to observe.

At the beginning of our discussion of *influence*, we incorporated the terms *self-motivation* and *self-actualization*. Our hypothesis is that subordinates are more likely to work harder to achieve organizational goals, in the most desirable manner, if they are a part of the decision-making process. Self-motivation is fairly simple; if one has a personal stake in reaching organizational goals, he will require less supervision, will be more likely to operate in an acceptable manner, and will sense a deeper feeling of achievement in reaching those goals. Self-motivation can occur from a variety of stimuli. Self-actualization is somewhat different in that it deals with an inner self. Abraham Maslow describes *self-actualization* as referring "to the desire for self fulfillment, namely, to the tendency for one to become actualized in what one is potentially."[12] Self-actualized, self-motivated people, then, are more likely to be influenced to do what is desired of them because of a personal commitment rather than because of a concern for authority or power.

Since World War II greater emphasis has been placed on attracting high-caliber young men into the police services. In 1967 the President's Commission on Law Enforcement and Administration of Justice focused attention on the need for formally educated police officers. "The ultimate aim of all police departments should be that all personnel with general enforcement powers have baccalaureate degrees."[13] High-ranking officers' objectives should be advanced degrees.

We concur with the commission's recommendations but foresee some administrative problems for those organizations that continue to operate with the traditional authoritarian model.

Maslow's theory takes on new and special meaning for police organizations. It appears likely that a better-educated young man will be more critical of the organization and of himself and less likely that he will be content to simply "carry out orders." There is a danger that police organizations, police managers, may not recognize the new type of recruit and may not use his *self-actualizing* needs properly. If this occurs, it can be anticipated that retention rate of our brightest resource will sharply decline, and today's problems will continue to be tomorrow's.

Reliance upon strict authoritarian controls may continue to insure respectable crime statistics, but as previously mentioned, these may not be a reliable barometer of organizational effectiveness.

Chapter Summary

In the preceding pages we have tried to show that organizations whose managers exercise poor control, or whose control is inconsistent at different levels, tend to have limited organizational effectiveness and, conversely, that organizations whose managers exercise proper control at every level tend to have a higher degree of organizational effectiveness. We have also explored three concepts of control: the use of authority, power, and influence, and we hope that all three emerged as legitimate and as having a direct and supportive relationship with each other. It should be obvious that we have leaned strongly toward the integration of the man and the organization. It is our belief that true high level police organizational effectiveness can be achieved only when each able human component of the organization is encouraged to make use of his personal influences.[14]

NOTES

1. The President's Commission on Law Enforcement and Administration of Justice *Task Force Report: The Police* (Washington, D. C.: Government Printing Office, 1967): pp. 28-30.
2. George D. Eastman and Esther M. Eastman, *Municipal Police Administration* (Washington, D. C.: International City Management Association 1969): pp. 20-21.
3. Manual of the Los Angeles Police Department (Los Angeles, Calif.: Los Angeles Police Department, 1970): IV, Chap. 2. Sec. 292.

4. Harold J. Leavitt. *Managerial Psychology,* 2nd ed. (Chicago: University of Chicago Press, 1958): pp. 171-173, 175.

5. *Ibid.,* p. 180.

6. John M. Pfiffner and Frank P. Sherwood, *Administrative Organization* (Englewood Cliffs, N.J.: Prentice-Hall, Inc., 1960): p. 75.

7. *Ibid.,* p. 25.

8. Warren G. Bennis, *Changing Organizations* (New York: McGraw-Hill Book Company, 1966): p. 168.

9. Pfiffner and Sherwood, *Administrative Organization,* pp. 310-11.

10. Rensis Likert, *New Patterns of Management* (New York: McGraw-Hill Book Company, 1961): p. 58. (For a more complete discussion of *influence* and *performance,* see pp. 44-60.)

11. Peter M. Blau and Richard W. Scott. *Formal Organizations* (San Francisco: Chandler Publishing Company, 1962): p. 140.

12. Abraham H. Maslow, *Motivation and Personality* (New York: Harper & Row, Publishers, 1954): pp. 91-92.

13. The President's Commission on Law Enforcement and Administration of Justice, *The Challenge of Crime in a Free Society* (Washington, D. C.: Government Printing Office 1967): p. 110.

14. The Learning Exercise is taken from J. William Pfeiffer and John E. Jones, *A Handbook of Structured Experiences for Human Relations Training* (Iowa City, Iowa: University City Associates Press, 1969), pp. 86-88.

Applied Perspectives

ORGANIZATION and administration have not simply emerged from the practical affairs of men. Whether they realize it or not, managers' theories and assumptions have often emerged from dialectic or philosophical issues. Practical men of affairs may jokingly dismiss the humanist and philosopher as naïve intellectuals but they are indebted to them nevertheless.

This section concerns itself with the practical application and development of power and authority in law enforcement. Understanding both theoretical and applied structures enables one to gain a broader perspective of law enforcement as a system and process. Some of the critical subjects raised in this section include:

The training of police officers
The philosophy of administration
The role of the policeman
Quality control in law enforcement
Variables which influence police officers
The problem of manpower
The consequences of police organization
Police administration
The use and abuse of power in law enforcement
The group dynamics of law enforcement

We urge the reader to reflect upon the following material with care, for the organization and application of law enforcement has firm roots in past theoretical considerations. Becker, Mann and Lubin present issues and concerns that will hopefully provide a foundation for further investigation and insight into the applied inner workings of power and authority in law enforcement.

6

HISTORICAL-PHILOSOPHICAL
DEVELOPMENT OF ADMINISTRATION*

Harold K. Becker

PHILOSOPHY has been interpreted in many ways. It might be understood as a love of wisdom; or a body of principles which would appeal to the scientific manager of administration; or a set of values involving the inquiries, debates, and verbiage of much administrative literature concerning the dichotomy of "is" and "ought"; or a view which could be related to the hue and cry for universal principles; or a field of study. For the purposes of this work and to develop topic parameters, philosophy is viewed as a system of ideas.[1] In dealing with systems it is necessary to categorize people, ideas, and issues. Three approaches are utilized which have been modified from their original source.[2]

1. a constitutional-legal rational philosophy forged from a framework of legal rights and obligations of government;
2. a structural-descriptive philosophy with its primary impetus coming from the scientific management area; and
3. the socio-psychological philosophy which stresses the systematic study of human behavior (beginning with the Hawthorne studies) in an organizational environment.

The above three divisions are not necessarily sharply divided but interact with, and react to, other systems and ideas as related to public administration.

Constitutional-Legal Approach

In 1887 Woodrow Wilson set a precedent for his contemporaries (and those to follow) with his views on the nature of adminis-

*Reprinted by permission of the author and publisher from *Issues in Police Administration* by Harold K. Becker (Metuchen, N. J.: Scarecrow Press, 1970). Copyright © 1970 by Harold K. Becker.

tration. Wilson's own philosophy, that man could remake society, added substantially to the reform and progressive period of
the 1900's. The reform and progressive movement appeared to
blend naturally with the concept of scientific methods in public
administration. Science became all-important, facts became
"sovereign".[3] Wilson wrote that administration is an area of business and that the object of administrative study is to obtain a
foundation laid deep in stable principle. He advocated the separation of politics and administration, asserting that administration
lies outside the proper sphere of politics and that administrative
questions are not political questions. Wilson, like Willoughby at
a later date, was legally oriented. Wilson emphasized that public
administration is the detailed and systematic execution of public
law. He was an early exponent of universal principles in dealing
with administration and a supporter of the concept of the
"science of administration."[4]

In writing *Politics and Administration* (1900), F. J. Goodnow
was also caught in the stream of progressivism. He may have been
influenced by Wilson's essay since he continued the idea of the
separation of administration and politics. Goodnow stressed the
concept that politics were detrimental to administrative efficiency. The separation of politics and administration is more
complex than stated above, however, and Goodnow found both
good and bad in separation. He indicated that it is impossible to
assign these functions to separate authorities because governmental power cannot be clearly divided.[5] Goodnow suggested a
possible solution: the assigning of a degree of control of administration by politics dependent upon the type of administration.
Administration could be of a judicial or governmental type. Politics should not be involved in justice. However, with regard to
government (the executive portion in particular), it must be subordinate to politics.[6]

W. F. Willoughby, who was legally oriented, discussed weaknesses in government administration and advocated scientific
principles of public administration. Willoughby continued the
Wilson-Goodnow concept of administration as being "apolitical". Like Goodnow, who was dissatisfied with the trichotomy
(executive, legislative, and judicial) dictum of democratic govern-

ment, Willoughby suggested five divisions of governmental power: executive, legislative, judicial, administrative, and electoral. Willoughby was concerned both with the dichotomy between administration and politics and with the fact that administration is a separate function from the executive role of government. He restated the claim for scientific sophistication in his *Principles of Public Administration* (1927). He took the position that there are fundamental principles analogous to those characterizing any science which can be determined by the application of the scientific method. Willoughby's contributions were multi-philosophical. He presented a discussion of the administration-politics dichotomy and then emphasized the administrative process as a technical and management attitude which should be used as a foundation for the legal involvement.[7]

Summary of the constitutional-legal philosophy. This system was a continuation of Constitutional legal opinion and decision based on legal rights and obligations of government. It emphasized the normative and political aspects of government. Wilson has been credited with focussing attention on public administration as an area of study in his essay "The Study of Administration" (1887). He emphasized that public administration is the detailed and systematic execution of public law and the separation of politics and administration.

Goodnow and later Willoughby continued the idea of the separation of administration from politics. Goodnow does indicate that governmental power cannot be clearly divided and that it becomes impossible to divert these functions to other authorities. Willoughby suggested five divisions of governmental power with equal importance on the administrative role.

Wilson and Goodnow, in rejecting the rationalism of nineteenth century political ideology of a system of legal literary theory and the paper pictures of the Constitution, introduced the concept of administration as apolitical. Simon, at a later period, developed a similar theory focussing on the separation of facts and values.

The major criticism of the constitutional-legal philosophy was its narrow approach to the study of administration.

Structural-Descriptive Approach

With the emphasis upon efficiency and scientific methodology the inquiry of administration retained the mantle of progressivism. Frederick W. Taylor represented the synthesization of scientific management in his *Shop Management* (1903) and *Principles of Scientific Management* (1910). Scientific management was the vehicle for a positivist attitude concerning the universality of management principles. Waldo has written that scientific management has contributed techniques and philosophy to the study and application of public administration.[8] Early contributors to the development of scientific management as applicable to public administration were: Henri Fayol, *Industrial and General Administration* (1930); V. A. Graicunas, "Relationship and Organization"; Gulick and Urwick, *Papers on the Science of Administration* (1937); and F. A. Cleveland, W. E. Mosher, and Frank Gilbreth. With the establishment of scientific management (efficiency and methodology) and the empirical investigation into principles, public administration assumed a new sophistication and direction. Among Taylor's contemporaries were persons interested in governmental reform such as Morris L. Cooke, who was employed in government service, Henry P. Kendall, who advocated governmental departmentalization according to functional management,[9] and Fayol, who applied scientific concepts toward the managerial or executive functions of administration. Waldo suggested that the philosophical development from the negative and moral to the positive and scientific attitude in personnel administration could be traced directly to scientific management.[10]

Leonard D. White gave direction to the philosophy in his definition of administration as organization and personnel management adjusted with financial and legal controls.[11] White, in his *Introduction to the Study of Public Administration* (1926), emphasized the structural and descriptive characteristics of administration. He viewed administration as not apolitical in his administrative history analyses: *The Federalists* (1948), *The Jeffersonians* (1951), *The Jacksonians* (1954), and *The Republican Era* (1958). In writing "The Meaning of Principles of Public

Administration''[12] White advocated the scientific approach to administration and suggested that principles are tested universal hypotheses. Possibly White's major force in relation to public administration is his role as structural-descriptive historian and his emphasis and definition of principles of administration.

Luther Gulick, together with Lyndall Urwick, continued the movement of scientific management into public administration. He carried the concept of work division of the "managers" into theories of departmentalization. In his "Notes on the Theory of Organization" he viewed governmental departments as being organized into divisions by purpose, with a further subdivision by process (finance, personnel, etc.). Gulick stressed the concept of efficiency as a basic good for public or private organizations. The operationalization of public administration was identified by Gulick (with its relationship to principles and universalism of Taylor and Fayol) by the mnemonic word POSDCORB which synthesized the scientific management approach. Urwick also presented the case for scientific management and dismissed the individual as being unimportant. Urwick's belief was in priority of organization structure with the necessary ingredients of planning and design which are all highly related to various types of principles. The organization came first, and man could be molded to fit the organization. In the *Papers on the Science of Administration,* Gulick and Urwick brought together a group of articles which expressed the attitude that public administration was nearing the position of a science in which values and ends could be put to one side. However, the seeds of discontent were also sown in the same publication, in two major essays: the first dealing with the Hawthorne study by Anderson, Whitehead, and Elton Mayo; and the second, an essay by Mary Parker Follett.

Herbert A. Simon has continued to a remarkable degree, though with some modifications, the application of science to public administration. Simon has stated the logical-positivist dictum that values can be removed from the science of public administration as they have been from the natural sciences. A true science is only concerned with fact. Simon has attacked the traditional concept of science, however, claiming that the so called principles are only proverbs which have not been based on

empirical research. This was not an attempt to eliminate principles but only a disagreement as to interpretation of fundamentals.
Simon stressed decision making, not the principles as indicated
by the *Papers*, as the heart of administration. The concept of
administration as apolitical came under attack since the separation of powers' position viewed administration as technical, and
therefore based on the principles.

Another important movement within the structural-
descriptive system was the President's Committee Report. This
report, published in 1937, emphasized the *Papers* by agreeing that
the foundations of effective management in public affairs are well
known. This gave respectability to governments' efforts to develop efficiency by the use of certain well-established principles.

Summary of the structural-descriptive philosophy. This system
emphasized the use of principles in describing public administration. Efficiency and scientific methodology were the framework
for the approach. The belief that administrative study could disregard values was accepted. The more articulate members of this
system were White, Gulick and Urwick. The major criticism of
this system was its lack of interest in people. Organization and
principles became paramount. Emphasis was placed on the
science of administration and the development of facts.

Socio-Psychological Approach

This third dimension to "systems that have influenced
thinking in public administration" was initiated by the classical
examples of the Hawthorne study by Mayo, Roethlisberger, and
Dickson; and by Mary Parker Follett's *Dynamic Administration*.
This particular system has been involved with man as the center
of inquiry in an administrative situation. As Pfiffner has indicated, this system has " . . . a set of values which is highly humani-
tarian, democratic, people-centered, and oriented in ideas of
social justice".[13] It was felt that the structural-descriptive system
with its lack of inquiry into values was cold and distant, and the
phrase "machine model" may be descriptively accurate.

As a result of the behavioral impetus in the area of public

administration, Simon, Smithburg, and Thompson have established their concept of administration as a social process. The authors constructed, on a psychological and sociological frame of reference, an explanation of public administration which was to be non-normative, free from values, desires, and prejudices, "a science in the sense of an objective understanding of the phenomena without confusion between facts and values."[14]

The behavioral approach views organization as a social group and work as a social activity. The individual brings to his work organization his mental as well as his physical identity. As well as the formal structure of the organization there exists an informal social structure that is dynamic, responsive, and capable of unknown power, which at times may be distinct from the formal organization.

From this social-dynamic approach, which moves away from the legalistic and mechanistic view of administration, inquiries of administration can be made which have greater breadth and depth. The following questions are indicative of this philosophical system:[15]

1. What is the social environment within which organizations, individuals, and varied combinations of individuals operate?
2. What persons and group affiliations influence attitudes and decisions?
3. How are human needs being met within the organization?
4. How will a proposed action be received by the individuals who occupy centers of informal authority?

The socio-psychological system brings together the elements of the behavioral sciences with their milieu of philosophy and mythology, and views public administration from many directions. The primary approach of this system is to stress the importance of empirical research and to find what is actually being done in administrative areas before universals are developed to describe public administration. Most of the principles have come under attack by a newer group of writers on public administration.[16]

Summary of the socio-psychological philosophy. The study of public administration under this system adopted the proposition that administration is a social process, rather than simply an exercise of authority and command, in terms of formal responsibilities and functions. The focus is now on relationships of people, processes, and patterns of communication. This system has moved away from the concept of formal organization, principles, and the legal foundation of administration. This sytem has taken an antimanagement position, and has attacked the traditionalists' parochial orientation based on POSDCORB and the machine model. The overview is that some kind of millennium has developed in the name of socio-psychological philosophy where there is a meeting of the legal, scientific manager, and socio-groups. The basic concepts of the past are coming into conflict with the empirical studies which are being directed into all areas of public administration. This shift in administrative thinking is not new. Dahl and Sayre stated in the *Public Administrative Review* (1950) that interest in public administration has moved from an emphasis upon science of administration to one of placing administration in its larger social bureaucratic setting.

Rationality as a Philosophical Question

Barrett, in the *Irrational Man*, expressed the view that human beings are irrational much if not all of the time. His primary thesis is that man has no alternative but to be irrational, since the situation in which human beings find themselves is essentially meaningless and absurd. To be rational presupposes that one can find some sense and meaning in things.

However, Veatch's view, in *Rational Man*, is that rationality is a defensible end or goal of man. It becomes an end which is not automatic and without criticism but nevertheless one based upon reason, and desired as a proper position.

Rationality is not a new concept to administrative students. In the constitutional-legal approach, which stressed the concepts of legal rights and obligations of government and the beginnings of a science, rationality took two forms: (1) rationality emphasized the power of human reason to understand the facts of human relationships and to manipulate relationships in logically determined ways to achieve predetermined goals, and (2) the role of the administrator was burdened with the use of techniques and principles in dealing with organization and especially in the concept of manipulation of organization.

The present approach to rationality in administration has changed in philosophy and has extended its parameters. The present position encompasses the rational and irrational factors in human envolvement. Rationality also considers inquiry concerning social factors which may influence reasoning. The newer rationality philosophy has subordinated the position of techniques and principles on the part of the administrator and his monocratic behavior, suggesting that "there are even beginnings of what might be called democratic administrative theory, in contrast to theory that has been authority oriented."[17]

The *Standard College Dictionary* defined rationality as: (1) the quality or condition of being rational; reasonableness; (2) the cause of reason; rationale; and (3) something rational, as an act, belief, practice, etc. In attempting to be more specific and provide a firmer foundation for administrative relationships Pfiffner defined rationality to mean " . . . the capacity of man to make choices based upon conscious deliberation about the means selected to achieve specified ends".[18]

Simon, in *Administrative Behavior*, defined rationality as "concerned with the selection of preferred behavior alternatives in terms of some system of values"[19] where the results of the behavior can be evaluated. Unlike Pfiffner's definition, which indicated the phenomenon of "conscious deliberation," Simon indicated that the selection of alternatives can be of a conscious or subconscious nature. Simon then redefined rationality to be related to specific situations:[20]

1. Objectively rational, if in fact it is the correct behavior, for maximizing given values in a given situation.
2. Subjectively rational, if it maximizes attainment relative to the actual knowledge of the subject.
3. Consciously rational, if it has made the adjustment of means to ends as in a conscious process.
4. Deliberately rational, if the adjustment of means to ends has been deliberately brought about by the individual or by the organization.
5. Organizationally rational, if it is oriented to the

organization's goals.

　　6. Personally rational, if it is oriented to the individual's goals.

　　Pfiffner's definition may be weak in that it deals with a conscious state of mind and neglects subconscious interactions in selecting the proper means to develop specific ends. Simon's multi-definition is also weak in that there is no universality of the concept of rationality but a fragmented approach depending on situation.

　　Pfiffner's definition will be modified to indicate selection of alternatives based upon conscious and subconscious deliberations about the means selected to achieve specific ends.

　　Having operationalized a definition of rationality it is now necessary to view the limits to which rationality can proceed. The crux of the problem of limitation lies within the means-ends phenomenon.

　　The ends to be obtained by the development of certain means will have the following relationships: (1) means available for selection will be limited; (2) means cannot be completely separated from ends; and (3) ends may be formally defined in terms of policy statements of an organization, whereas means are generally more flexible although limited. The analogy can be drawn between economic man and administrative man in that both these concepts of rational behavior are held constant in dealing with means and ends. Rational behavior would find axiomatic the following three conditions:[21] (1) to view all the alternatives prior to making the decision; (2) to consider all the alternatives to choice with their many complex systems; and (3) to select a system of values as criteria, singling out one from a complete set of alternatives.

　　Simon agrees with the above description of real behavior being dominated by irrational sequences. He did indicate that behavior reveals segment of rationality but that there is little interaction between these bits and pieces of rational indulgences. Simon has described limits of rationality to be functional in three areas: knowledge, value, and behavior.[22]

　　1. Rationality requires complete knowledge and anticipation
　　　　of end results which will follow each choice. Knowledge of
　　　　end results, however, is not always complete. Rationality

implies a complete knowledge of end results and consequences for each choice. In actual practice ability to know the maximum data concerning a particular end result might be analogous to geometric progression. As pieces of information, related to the original phenomenon, are brought together, new decisions might be made with the necessity of making new choices and obtaining additional knowledge. In actuality, complete knowledge concerning a phenomenon is seldom obtained. Knowledge is generally related to time, effort, and funds. The longer the time period a phenomenon can be investigated, the greater the effort made by personnel; and adequate funds available will relate directly to the obtainable knowledge.

2. Since consequences lie in the future, imagination must supplement the lack of experience of similar situations. Anticipation can only partially be imagined since related values are attached to nonexistent situations. Simon indicates that an experience which is anticipated may be very different from the realization of the situation. This relates not only to the failure to anticipate end results but also to a lack of mental ability to focus on a particular end result in its entirety. Attention will drift from sets of values or subunits of values relating to one end result to other sets of values relating to different end results. There are limiting factors in imagining end results and assigning values to them.

3. Rationality requires a choice among all possible alternative behaviors. Only a small number of possible behaviors will be reviewed for selection. In actuality an array of possible patterns of behavior exist, consciously as well as unconsciously, which will have three stages of involvement: mental processes which accept, store, and relate to patterns of behavior; physical processes which might be related to reflex actions and unconscious physical manipulations; and biological processes which are occurrences of tissue reproduction and cell division which receive no formal direction from the mental processes. Of all these pattern processes only a few appear to be possible behavior alternatives which can be placed in a position of choice.

Simon has indicated that the primary concern of administrative theory is "with the boundary between the rational and the nonrational aspects of human social behavior."[23] The limits of rationality are concerned with human activity which satisfies rather than maximizes. Economic man attempts to maximize his ends based on rational choice while administrative man accepts solutions which are lesser in degree than the concept of maximization. Simon also makes the comparison between economic man who deals with the world and administrative man who he says deals with something less than the real world. Administrative man considers the real world as "empty and that facts of the real world have no great relevance to any particular situation he is facing."[24] Administrative man develops simplified models which take into account just a few of the factors that are felt to be most relevant. The major characteristics of administrative man according to Simon, are:[25]

1. A tendency to satisfy, rather than maximize, by making choices without examining all possible behavior alternatives;
2. Ignores the interrelatedness of behavior and means-ends;
3. Makes decision with relatively simple rules of thumb that do not make impossible demands upon capacity for thought.

Summary concerning limits of rationality as a philosophical question. Rationality as a man-goal is expressed in this paper as reflecting an end result which is based upon reason and is desired as a proper position. A modified definition of rationality was derived from Pfiffner's and Simon's approach to rationality and is expressed as the selection of alternatives based on conscious and subconscious deliberations about the means selected to achieve specific ends. There is general agreement among writers on public administration as to the limitations of rationality. Limitations have been grouped into three primary areas: knowledge, which is not always complete because of the sheer magnitude of information which may relate directly and indirectly to a particular end result; value distribution, which will alternate between end results and expectations which correspond to values attached to nonexistent situations; and behavior, which will be limited because of the magnitude of patterns of behavior which would theoretically be considered. Therefore, the limits of rationality are directly related to the inability of the human mind to focus on a single situation with all the possible alternatives of knowledge, value, and behavior that would be necessary to make a choice from available alternatives.

Rationality and the Decision-Making Process

Nicolaidis, in his *Policy-Decision and Organization Theory*,[26] interpreted decision-making as something different from the traditional concepts of rationality. He related orthodox concepts of rationality to economic man, engineering man, and the scientific method where all relevant facts are obtained and a selection is made from an array of end results. This system excluded human prejudice and bias which might influence the decision. Nicolaidis attempted to go beyond the orthodox concept and attempted to operationalize social factors which interact with, and influence the facts, and in turn present facts of their own. Nicolaidis appears to travel farther than Simon in the direction of making social data accountable in the decision making process.

Banfield's description of a decision making process can be used as an example of the orthodox approach to rational decision making:[27]

1. The decision maker lists the opportunities for action open to him.
2. He identifies the consequences that would follow from the adoption of each of the possible actions.
3. He selects the action that would lead to the preferred set of consequences.

Banfield further suggests that "for practical purposes, a rational decision is one in which alternatives and consequences are considered as fully as the decision ... given the time and other resources available ...."[28] The contrast between Nicolaidis and Banfield is apparent. The former is influenced by a myriad of social factos which influence decisions and the latter takes as a premise a mechanical, automated approach.

In describing the decision-process Nicolaidis suggested that there was a continuum of decision making models varying from classical rationality at one extreme to intuition at the other. Within this continuum there exists a plurality of values:[29]

1. A decision must have some degree of conformity with the personal interests, values, and benefits of the decision maker.
2. It should meet the value yardsticks of superiors.
3. It should be acceptable to those who are affected as well as those charged with its implementation.
4. It should be reasonable within its context.
5. It should contain built-in justification which will furnish an excuse, and possibly an avenue of retreat, if case results are not as anticipated.

In moving away from orthodoxy in administrative rationality an array of social phenomena becomes suspect. Concepts such as emotions, politics, power, group dynamics, personality, and mental health become worthy of inquiry or, at least, of recognition that they exist if nothing more than as unknowns. Behavioral science information assumes a relative position among the data in developing a solution to a particular problem. A broader base is used to develop solutions to particular problems.

The decision making processes have been found as entities in five approaches or views in categorizing decision making. The five approaches would be: a mental process, a social process, an organizational process, a general problem-solving process, and a specific problem process.[30]

1. A mental process utilizes the choice of alternative possibilities and the mental characteristics which bring about a choice. Simon's trichotomy of knowledge, value, and behavior would be characteristic of the mental process.
2. In the social process decisions are made in a social setting by individual thinking which is related to social influence, or by interaction within a group process. The primary characteristic of this process is that decisions are recognized as being made in a social setting interacting with individual values and goals.
3. An organizational process is in part a subdivision of a social process. However, since it is such a large division of the social process, it has been set aside and is dealt with as a

specific function of the social process.

4. A general problem-solving process gives emphasis to techniques of selecting alternative solutions. It is also an attempt to develop a general theory which is applicable in selecting alternative end results regardless of knowledge, value, and behavior involved.

5. A specific problem-solving process emphasizes the process of developing specific categories of decisions such as personnel decisions, economic decisions, etc.; and the development of a general theory which is applicable to the specific category.

In Simon's approach decision making is the heart of administration. A decision is defined as a conclusion drawn from a set of premises. Premises are of two kinds: (1) facts, and (2) values. The validity of facts can be determined by empirical propositions. Values are imperatives; they have to do with oughts and they cannot be empirically validated. They are neither true nor untrue in any empirical sense.

Summary of rationality and the decision making process. Traditional concepts of rational decision making accept man as an individual who maximizes his position by making a determined valuation of all possible factors which relate to a particular problem and then selects the best choice from an array of end results. Examples of this phenomenon would be administrative man, engineering man, and economic man. Economic theory has reinforced the image of man as a rational creature. Economic theory is concerned with a rational man who would save his money, spend wisely, and generally exhibit predictable behavior in the area of economic choice.[31]

The traditional concept excludes social factors of an unconscious as well as a conscious nature. Human bias which might influence the decision is not considered. This type of decision making is mechanical and appeals to the scientific management concept of efficiency, economy, and selection of a one best way.

In contrast to the traditional rational concept in dealing with decisions is a move toward the consideration of an array of social factors which might influence a decision. Simon and, to a greater degree, Nicolaidis have directed much attention to this approach.

Nicolaidis indicates that decision making is not a single process but can be attributed to several independent processes: social, mental, and organizational.

In the practical application of decision making, fact and value are organically related and incapable of separation. Simon's purpose was to view decision making by isolating characteristics of the process for purposes of analysis and to develop an ideal type.

Attempts to Formulate a Theory of Rationality in Decision Making

Attempts to formulate theories relative to rationality are not new or confined to writers on public administration. John Dewey (1859-1952) is one of the significant writers who examined rationality outside the fortress of public administration. His philosophy held that the characteristics of human activity are instruments for solving psychological and social problems. He postulated that value propositions can be arrived at by the power of human reason. He recognized unconscious motivation and related this to the concept of habit. The concept of unconscious motivation dates back to Spinoza (1632-1677), Leibniz (1646-1716), and Freud (1856-1939). The evolution of ethical thought is characterized by the fact that value judgments concerning human conduct were made in reference to the motivations underlying the act rather than to the act itself.[32] The main emphasis in Dewey's position is one of the relationship between means and ends as the empirical basis for the validity of norm. The end, to Dewey, is merely a series of acts viewed at a remote stage, and means merely represent the series viewed at an earlier one. The end is the last act thought of, the means are the acts to be performed prior to it in time. Means and ends are two names for the same reality.[33]

Simon pursued the concept of means-end as being merely a continuum in which ends have a hierarchical arrangement. The means-end hierarchy has three primary limitations:[34]

1. The ends to be attained by the choice of a particular behavior alternative are often incomplete or incorrectly stated through failure to consider the alternative ends that could be reached by selection of another behavior.
2. In actual situations a complete separation of means from

ends is usually impossible, for the alternative means are not usually valuationally neutral.
3. The means-end terminology tends to obscure the role of the time element in decision making.

The concept of means-ends is to maximize satisfaction of needs with a minimum disposal of means. As Nicolaidis has indicated, this is the concept of the economic principle " ... which is identical with the concept of rationality. Rationality has been considered as the administrative version of the economic principle."[35] The economic principle is formulated around two concepts: (1) unlimited ends, and (2) limited means.

Dewey's concept of means-ends as a validity of norms has been expanded to include Simon's limitations and modified to be a phenomenon of administrative rationality as analogous to economic concepts. Therefore, in developing a theory of rationality, it is necessary to view the relationship of means-end to the total view of rationality.

In an attempt to move away from rationality based on economic principles of ends and means, consideration should be given to two ideal types:[6] (1) the fourfold model of the real social man; and (2) the model of the rationalized organizational man.

The fourfold model can be divided into the area of expected rational behavior which considers the facts which the decision maker knows and can evaluate himself, and the area dealing with anticipated nonrational behavior which considers value judgments and factors which are either unknown or which the decision maker cannot evaluate by himself. The emphasis of the fourfold model is the acceptance of man's being irrational. Realizing this, man can adjust himself to a systematic approach to decision making and therefore become rational. The shift is away from man and toward the system into which man must fit in order to be rational in solving problems.

The second model, which deals with the rationalized organization man, can be divided into three primary areas: (1) the area of expected natural rationality which deals with known facts which the decision maker can evaluate by his own computational capacities and a consideration of factual judgments expected to be naturally rational; (2) an area of improved rationality which considers unknown factors that the decision maker can evaluate by using staff work, computers, statistics, probabilities, etc.; and (3) an area of controlled rationality which deals with value judgment controlled and predetermined by given policies. This approach has been criticized by Melman[37] as being an extension of the "one best way" and as mythology from the traditionalist concept of industrial engineering. He also indicated that from a mathematical point of view the one best way is not justifiable.

Rationality theory has been attacked by Simon as developing a notion of a man who never existed since "the capacity of the human mind for formulating and solving complex problems is very small compared with the size of problems whose solution is required for objectively rational behavior in the real world."[38] An argument in favor of rationality theory is the view that theoretical models are necessary as ideal types which describe rational behavior. It is not the purpose here to recommend an ideal model as a working entity but only to suggest that it represent certain characteristics which relate to the concept of administrative rationality. Weber's formulation of bureaucracy consists of such an ideal type. In Weber's attempt to develop his concept of bureaucracy there also develops an aura of rationality and, as indicated by Pfiffner, "Perhaps the major characteristic of the ideal type of bureaucracy is its effort to achieve rationality."[39]

In attempting to formulate theories of rationality as related to decision making it is necessary to further describe: (1) the classical model; (2) the normative model; and (3) the behavioral model.

The classical model of rationality has been described by March and Simon as the machine model. This assumption is derived from the mechanical attitude toward human motivation and behavior which, according to this view, is primarily related to self-interest. The machine model stressed the means-end relationship as one in which the decision maker analyzes the ends and then selects the means which are necessary to obtain the end goal. This Machiavellian view ignores the necessity of values except those of self-interest in that decisions are "completely independent of ethics, that a ruler serving the ends of his state can do no wrong."[40] The emphasis in the classical model is the maximization of self-interest. This approach is characteristic of formal logic, pure reasoning, and the application of scientific methodology. Classical decision making attempted to solve problems by looking for the one best way of rational man. In contrast, the behaviorist selected ideal types which emphasized major characteristics of decision making.

The normative model moves away from the mechanistic model in that it suggests "oughts," or what should be. A normative model is one that accepts a principle or action which is binding upon the members of a group and serves to guide, control, or regulate proper and acceptable behavior. The normative model of rationality is not necessarily based upon any scientific inquiry or hypothesis. The normative model may be of a minority view which is in conflict with the total group view relating to ought and should concepts. A normative view is also related to some agreement of what is good and what is bad. When principles of good and bad have been resolved, the normativist can deal with oughts in normative terms. However, it is felt by some that the questions of good-bad, right-wrong, are concepts which defy definitive agreement.

The behavioral model of rationality attempts in a systematic way to describe, measure, and predict human behavior. The decision maker is still dealing in part with self-interest realities but is willing to compromise to obtain the end result. However, in compromising, there may be a shift to a less desirable end result. The administrative decision maker who assumes the behavioral model approach of give-and-take by dealing with and anticipating human behavior is involved in the area of administrative politics, according to Pfiffner.[41] Behavioral models deal with areas of intuition, objective analysis, indecisiveness, administrative leadership and authoritarian leadership, while the classical models were concerned with factual decision making, charismatic leadership, and decisiveness.

Summary of attempts to formulate a theory of rationality in decision making. Spinoza, Leibniz, and Freud were among the first to inquire into the unconscious acts of man. Dewey continued inquiry into unconscious motivation of man in making decisions. His main emphasis was on the relationship between means and ends. He felt the end was a minor factor in a series of means. Simon also pursued the concept of means-end as being a continuum in which ends were at the top level of a hierarchy. The means-end phenomenon is faulty because it is based on incomplete information; a complete separation of means-end is impossible, and the time element is often not considered in ideal types of decision making. The basic concept of means-end is to maximize satisfaction of needs with a minimum disposal of means: (1) unlimited ends, and (2) limited means.

Theories of rationality were related to three descriptive models: the classical model, the normative model, and the behavioral model. The classical model attempted to solve problems by looking for the one best way of rational man. In contrast, the behavioralist selected ideal types which emphasized major characteristics of decision making. The behavioral model dealt with areas of intuition and objective analysis. The normative model was one that accepts a principle or action which is binding on the members of a group and serves to guide and control.

Values Implicit In Such Theories

Rationality of decision making suggests that thinking about what is desirable and right can be systematic and directed into action.

Philosophies of other generations have declared various concepts relating to rationality and the universality of standards. Philosophers have developed a value framework in dealing with standards.

The nineteenth-century philosophers were skeptical about universal values and the impracticability of the concept "that every person already knew in his heart what was right, and that the conscience, moral sense, or reason of all humanity was identical."[42] The trend was away from universal standards, and criticism by Hegel and Marx in dealing with nationalism and class-struggle theory gave emphasis to this skepticism.

However, in the early years of the twentieth century Nietzsche called for a " ... re-valuation of all values and the pragmatists were insisting that there are no problems in general, hence, there could be no principles that solved all problems."[43]

In an attempt to move away from a universal approach philosophers developed a logical positivism concept which made a distinction between facts and values. The assertion is made that values can be removed from facts by decision makers in solving problems. The comparison is generally made between the natural scientist and his ability to eliminate value in the laboratory, and the approach of the social scientist in the field with his efforts to eliminate value in his studies.

Mailick, in *Concepts and Issues in Administrative Behavior*, has identified six standards which, if viewed independently, have the characteristics of a universal. These values are listed below with the names of individuals who believed each standard represented a complete universal system:

1. *Happiness*; which can also be described in terms of desirable results, maximized satisfactions, and efficiency. Writers who believed in happiness as a universal were Epicurus (341-270 B.C.) who developed a theory of life, defined philosophy as the art of making life happy, with intellectual pleasure or serenity the only good; Jeremy Bentham (1748-1832) who advocated the greatest happiness for the greatest number; and John Stuart Mill (1806-1873) who determined that universals were related to inductive reasoning.

2. *Lawfulness*; which would include precedents, customs, contracts, and authorizations. A writer who believed in lawfulness was Thomas Aquinas (1225-1274) who felt that reasoning starts with sense data.

3. *Harmony*; which might include logical consistency, platonic justice, order, plan, and common good. Writers who believed in harmony as a universal were Plato (428/427-348/347 B.C.) who investigated the development of a rational moral personality; and Immanuel Kant (1724-1804) whose *Critique of Pure Reason* opposed the concept that human intelligence has powers to arrive by pure thought at truths about entities which in their nature can never be objects of experience.

4. *Survival*; political power, and effect on friend-foe relations. A writer who believed in survival as a universal was Thomas Hobbes (1588-1679) who felt it was necessary to give every-

one a guarantee of the good behavior of his fellows by creating a power sufficient to keep them in awe.

5. *Integrity*; which could be described as self-respect, the rationality of the individual, and peace of mind. Writers who believed in integrity as a universal were Epictetus who viewed the world as a whole; Baruch Spinoza (1632-1677) who, regarding the world as a whole which would render it completely intelligible, attempted to build a mathematical philosophy filled with geometric axioms, postulates, and theories; and George Santayana (1863-1952) who, in *The Life of Reason*, advocated that reason is based on instinct which has become reflective and enlightened.

6. *Loyalty*; institutional trends and social causes. Writers who believed in loyalty as a universal were Georg Wilhelm Hegel (1770-1831) who, in *The Encyclopaedia of the Philosophical Science*, stated that reason can be related to logic, nature, and the mind; Karl Marx (1818-1883) who, besides his more renowned work, wrote *The Poverty of Philosophy* (1847) as an interpretation of economic history; and Josian Royce (1855-1916) who stated that scientific laws can be used as statistical formulas for behavior.

Mailick suggests that there is no universal value but many values which relate to the decision-making process. He further denies the universalist approach in this statement: "No one rule, no one goal, no one system sums up human wisdom."[44] He goes further to indicate that a decision-maker

> ... may make a very different evaluation of the contemplated action, if he asks himself how the action looks from another point of view, particularly from the standpoint that is diametrically opposite his present view (harmony as opposed to survival, lawfulness as opposed to happiness, and integrity as opposed to loyalty).[45]

Generally, decision-making has been performed as a one-sided, partial, incomplete operation; it has not involved criticism of some values which are important and permanent parts of the decision-maker's personality and culture.

Nicolaidis has also suggested that decisions are not based on a single standard or value but rather must meet many values, and has outlined five areas in which values become apparent in decision making.[46]

Summary of values implicit in such theories. The topic of values in making rational decisions has been a source of discussion from Plato and Epicurus to the present writers of public administration. There has been little agreement as to the role of values in decision making. An outstanding discourse on this conflict is that presented by Simon and Waldo, the former suggesting a value-free approach, the latter negating the separation of facts and values. Simon has modified the concept of earlier philosophers to move away from a universalist position and develop a logical positivist attitude which makes a distinction between facts and values. Nicolaidis has also suggested that decisions are not independent from values but suggests that there are many values which influence facts and the eventual decision.

Conclusions

Three approaches were utilized in this chapter which have been modified from their original source: (1) a constitutional-legal rational philosophy forged from a framework of legal rights and obligations of government, emphasizing the normative and political aspects and the detailed and systematic execution of public law and the separation of politics and administration. The major criticism of the constitutional-legal philosophy was its narrow approach to the study of administration. (2) A structural-descriptive philosophy, with its primary impetus coming from the scientific management era which emphasized the use of principles in describing public administration in a framework of efficiency and scientific methodology. This system is also narrow with its singular direction concerning principles, facts and efficiency. (3) The socio-psychological philosophy which stresses the systematic study of human behavior and which views organization as a social group and work as a social activity. This system has taken an anti-management position, and has attacked the traditionalists and their parochial orientation based on POSD-CORB and the machine model.

Rationality is not a new concept in administrative studies. In the constitutional-legal approach rationality took two forms: (1) rationality emphasized the power of human reason to understand the facts of human relationships and to manipulate relationships in logically determined ways to achieve predetermined goals; and (2) the role of the administration was burdened with the use of techniques and principles in dealing with organization and especially in the concept of manipulation of organization. A definition of rationality would indicate selection of alternatives based upon conscious and subconscious deliberations about the means selected to achieve specific ends. The problem of limitation lies within the means-ends phenomenon.

The ends to be obtained by the development of certain means will have the following relationships: (1) means available for selection will be limited; (2) means cannot be completely separated from ends; and (3) ends may be formally defined in terms of policy statements of an organization whereas means are generally more flexible although limited. Rational behavior would find axiomatic the following conditions: (1) to view all the alternatives prior to making the decision, (2) consider all the alternatives to choice with their many complex systems, and (3) select a system of values as criterion singling out one from a complete set of alternatives. Simon has described limits of rationality to be functional in three areas: knowledge, value, and behavior.

The limits of rationality are concerned with human activity which satisfies rather than maximizes. Economic man attempts to maximize his ends based on rational choice while administrative man satisfies and accepts solutions which are lesser in degree than the concept of maximization. Administrative man in satisfying develops simplified models which take into account just a few of the factors that are felt to be most relevant.

In describing rationality and the decision-process there was a continuum of decision making models varying from classical rationality at one extreme to intuition at the other. Within this continuum there exists a plurality of values.

In Simon's approach decision making is the heart of administration. A decision is defined as a conclusion drawn from a set of premises. Premises are of two kinds: (1) facts and (2) values. The validity of facts can be determined by empirical propositions.

Values are imperatives; they have to do with oughts and they cannot be empirically validated. They are neither true nor untrue in any empirical sense.

In attempts to formulate a theory of rationality the end has been considered as merely a series of acts viewed at a remote stage, and means merely represent the series viewed at an earlier one. The end is the last act thought of, the means are the acts to be performed prior to it in time. The concept of means-ends is to maximize satisfaction of needs with a minimum disposal of means. In developing a theory of rationality, it is necessary to view the relationship of means-end to the total view of rationality. Examples of two ideal types of rationality are: the fourfold model of the real social man, and the model of the rationalized organization man. Rationality theory has been attacked by Simon in that it develops a concept of a man who never existed.

Values in rationality of decision making suggest that thinking about what is desirable and right can be systematic and directed into action. In an attempt to move away from a universalist approach philosophers developed a logical positivist concept which made a distinction between facts and values. Six values have been identified and have been viewed independently as universal: happiness, lawfulness, harmony, survival, integrity, and loyalty. Nicolaidis has suggested that decisions are not based on a single standard or value but rather must meet many values. He suggests five areas in which values become apparent in decision making.

NOTES

1. Stover, Carl F., "Changing Patterns in the Philosophy of Management", *Public Administration Review*, Winter, 1958, p. 21.
2. Pfiffner, John M. and Presthus, Robert V., *Public Administration* (New York: The Ronald Press, 1960), p. 7.
3. *The Administrative State* (New York: The Ronald Press, 1948).
4. Wilson, Woodrow, 'The Study of Administration", *Political Science Quarterly*, December, 1941, pp. 493-504.
5. *Op. cit.*, Waldo, p. 16.
6. *Ibid.*, p. 79.
7. Willoughby wrote *The Government of Modern States* (1919), *Principles of Judicial Administration* (1929), *Principles of Legislative Organization and Administration* (1934).

8. *Op. cit.*, Waldo, p. 47.

9. *Op. cit.*, Pfiffner, p. 191.

10. *Op. cit.*, Waldo, p. 59.

11. *Op. cit.*, Pfiffner, p. 90.

12. Gaus, John M., White, Leonard D., and Dimock, Marshall E., *The Frontiers of Public Administration* (Chicago: University of Chicago Press, 1936).

13. *Op. cit.*, Pfiffner.

14. Simon, Herbert A., Smithburg, Donald W., and Thompson, Victor A., *Public Administration* (New York: Alfred A. Knopf, Inc., 1950).

15. Stover, Carl F., "Changing Patterns in the Philosophy of Management," *Public Administration Review*, Winter 1950, Vol. 18, Num. 1., pp. 21-27.

16. A few of the names which have become associated with the "new" group would include but not be restricted to: Robert K. Merton, *Reader in Bureaucracy*; Daniel Lerner and Harold D. Lasswell, The Policy Sciences; Rensis Likert, *Developing Patterns of Management*; Sam A. Stouffer, et al., *The American Soldier*; Chester I. Barnard, *The Functions of the Executive*; Talcott Parsons and Edward A. Shills, *Toward a General Theory of Action*; and Peter M. Blau, *The Dynamics of Bureaucracy*, to name a few.

17. Waldo, Dwight, *Ideas and Issues in Public Administration* (New York: McGraw-Hill, 1953), p. 104.

18. *Op. cit.*, Pfiffner, p. 116.

19. Simon, Herbert A., *Administrative Behavior* (New York: The Macmillan, 1945), p. 75.

20. *Ibid.*, pp. 76-77.

21. *Ibid.*, p. 80.

22. *Ibid.*, p. 81.

23. *Ibid.*, p. xxiv.

24. *Ibid.*, p. xxv.

25. *Ibid.*, p. xxvi.

26. Nicolaidis, Nicholas G., *Policy-Decision and Organization Theory* (University of Southern California Bookstore, John W. Donner Memorial Fund, Publication No. 11, 1960).

27. Banfield, Edward C., "Ends and Means in Planning," *Concepts and Issues in Administrative Behavior* (Englewood Cliffs, N.J.: Prentice Hall Inc., 1962), edited by Sidney Mailick and Edward H. Van Ness, p. 71.

28. *Ibid.*, p. 71.

29. *Op. cit.*, Nicolaidis

30. *Op. cit.*, Nicolaidis, pp. 36-42.

31. Simon, Herbert A., "Recent Advances in Organization Theory," *Research Frontiers in Politics and Government*, S. Bailey, editor (Washington, D. C.: Brookings Institution, 1955), pp. 32-35.

32. Mullahy, Patrick, "Values, Scientific Method and Psychoanalysis," *Psychiatry*, May, 1943.

33. Dewey, John, *Human Nature and Conduct* (New York: The Modern

Library, Random House, 1930), p. 34.
34. *Ibid., Administrative Behavior*, pp. 62-66.
35. *Op. cit.*, Nicolaidis, pp. 99-102.
36. *Ibid.*, pp. 103-7.
37. Melman, Seymour, *Decision-Making and Productivity* (New York: John Wiley and Sons, 1958), p. v.
38. Simon, Herbert A., *Models of Man-Social and Rational* (New York: John Wiley and Sons, 1957), p. 198.
39. *Op. cit.*, Pfiffner, p. 44.
40. March, James G., and Simon, Herbert A., *Organizations.* (New York: John Wiley and Sons, 1958).
41. *Op cit., Administrative Rationality*, p. 131.
42. Mailick, Sidney and Van Ness, E. H., *Concepts and Issues in Administrative Behavior* (Englewood Cliffs, N.J.: Prentice-Hall Inc., 1962), p. 82.
43. *Ibid.*, p. 82.
44. *Ibid.*, p. 89.
45. *Ibid.*, p. 88.
46. Pfiffner, John M., "Administrative Rationality," *Public Administration Review*, Spring 1960, Vol. 10, no. 2, p. 129.

7

PSYCHOLOGY OF POLICE ORGANIZATION: REWARD STRUCTURE AND GROUP DYNAMICS*

Phillip A. Mann

> Habit is habit, and not to be flung out of the window by any man, but coaxed downstairs a step at a time.
>
> —Mark Twain

IN the past, behavioral scientists have tended to view police behavior as a function of intrapersonal traits; such as, authoritarianism, sadism, psychopathy.[1] These trait examples also suggest psychologists' tendency to study such behavior as though it were a clinical problem. However, recent developments in psychology in general, and the increasing contact between behavioral scientists and policemen in particular, have shown more concern with role-related organizational and social system factors in police behavior. Among these are the systems of psychological and material incentives, and the regularly occurring reinforcing effects of work experience in an organization which are designated by the term reward structure.

The general concept of reward structure in organizations has been reviewed by Katz and Kahn (1964). The discussion here will deal with the topic as it has manifested itself in the author's experiences in working as a consultant to police departments. This is done in an effort to illuminate and make specific some of the ways in which reward structures affect the behavior of members of this social institution.

Perhaps an intrapsychic view of police work has been tenable because the rewards of police work are not highly visible and their work has been generally regarded as low in status and in pay.[2]

---

*Reprinted by permission of the publisher from Psychological Consultation with a Police Department by Philip A. Mann (Springfield, Ill.: Charles C Thomas, 1973). Copyright ©Charles C Thomas, 1973.

This assumption overlooks such concepts as adaptation-level (Helson, 1964), and implies that rewards can be encompassed exhaustively within the categories of pay and status or the gratification of personal, often socially undesirable, needs which could not be satisfied in other occupations or settings. Moreover, it is reasonable to argue that some behavioral traits are the result of, rather than a basis for attraction to, police work (Mann, 1971).

Another aspect of the historical view that may be a compelling reason for an intrapsychic perspective is the perception of police organizations as quasi-military in character. This concept provides a ready, but perhaps too facile, complementarity to such timehonored subjects of study in psychology as needs for order, conformity, and, of course, authoritarianism. There are some important differences, however, in the implications of the term military for the *real* military and the police organization, such as in the observance and legal status of limits on fraternization and discrimination by rank, and the separation of career tracks for officers and enlisted men in the armed services. Perhaps a better term for the police is semi-military, or better, hierarchical. In any case, this comparison is worth pursuing further from the standpoint of its organizational implications alone.

Incentives and Rewards

The military aspects of police organization are indeed authentic; that is to say, real; but they are not sufficient to explain police behavior or police department operations entirely. One important element of a reward-structure is promotion and advancement. Here, police departments differ from the military in several important respects.

The promotional capability of a police department is typically dependent on position vacancies, and there is a definite fixed correspondence between rank, pay and position. In the military, the rank of a person filling a particular slot may vary across several grades, promotions are based on time-in-grade and supervisor-initiated efficiency reports, and persons given a rank higher than that authorized for their position can be transferred laterally to another organization. Moreover, since the minimum twenty-year retirement option in the military probably creates more turnover at the top than is true in police departments, the military would seem to enjoy an advantage in both position openings and promotional capacity. Thus, a police department's ability to provide positive incentives such as promotions is dependent on the uncontrollable occurrence of vacancies. On the other hand, promotions must occur when vacancies occur whether or not there is a deserving candidate. Even assuming that there is always a deserving candidate, this form of reward is quite remote from any specific job performance.

In addition, the promotional machinery of a police department is typically tied to a civil service system wherein written examinations are given much higher weightings than are supervisor's evaluations. The consequences of this arrangement are that promotions probably reward intelligence primarily and not necessarily competent performance. Thus, the supervisor is left with little reward power for his subordinates and probably little incentive for providing supervision except for preventing gross violations of policy or incompetent performance through the imposition of negative sanctions; e.g., reprimand, suspension.

Other consequences follow. An organization with limited positive reward power may also be inclined to minimize the tendency to employ negative sanctions as a means of maintaining organizational balance and minimizing organizational strain. Individuals can help to maintain this system if supervisors are not informed of any more than is necessary (cf. Bittner, 1970). Given limited opportunities for advancement, this system virtually assures that there will be a high attrition rate of competent people at the lower ranks. The more competent an individual, the more likely he is to have alternative job opportunities available to him outside the department. While some of the more competent will be rewarded, the others may encounter frustration and the psychological incentives for leaving the department would be increased (Thibaut and Kelley, 1959). This situation would tend to make persistence in police work less a function of high competence than of dedication and group identification. Within these limitations, what is rewarded? Although it has been estimated that no more than 20 percent of a policeman's work involves detecting and apprehending criminals, and that the remainder is spent in providing service and assistance with various human problems (Bard, 1968), virtually 100 percent of the rewards are assigned according to the policeman's record in dealing with criminal activity.

Thus, an officer who may have saved lives through a successful family disturbance intervention, an officer who may have prevented a racial disturbance because he regularly socializes with and befriends minority group youth, or an officer who understandingly and patiently prevents a suicide through sympathetic listening to a person's troubles, may be rated as substandard if his record does not reflect a sufficient number of arrests and summonses. It may be *all in a day's work*, but it is not all in another day's pay. Usually a police department does not have an adequate reporting and accounting system for these acts of quiet human heroism, which speaks of their general valuation in police work and makes systematic reward for their performance all the more unlikely.

This system of limited tangible rewards and selective partial reinforcement tends to generate a strong group dynamic in which a policeman who intends to remain on the job must seek his rewards and guide his behavior on the basis of the group cohesiveness and the social norms which that group creates. These forces are probably the strongest ones regulating police behavior and deserve careful examination.

Group Dynamics

In work with police departments, some persistent and interesting phenomena of police group behavior have been observed from which inferences about group dynamics can be drawn. In the light of the previous discussion, it can be assumed that these processes will continue to influence a policeman's behavior when he is not in the immediate physical presence of his peers.

It is helpful in understanding the background of these processes to make comparisons with the behavior of workers who share similar conditions of socioeconomic status and organization of labor (Lipset, 1969); Sterling and Watson, 1970). Thus, the tendency for policemen to have primarily other policemen as social acquaintances is understood better as a characteristic shared with other workers whose labor is organized into shift work than as a result of any personal propensity for aloofness or clannishness, or because of defensiveness (see Westley, 1970). Similarly, it has been observed that many policemen are personally somewhat shy and hesitant in relating to persons of different socioeconomic status, but this behavior is not characteristic of their other relationships.

These forces at once tend to reduce the policeman's contacts as an autonomous participant in the on-going norm-generating social processes in the larger community, to create ambiguity for them about behavioral norms which are prevalent in the community, and to necessarily force the policeman to rely on social and behavioral prescriptions emanating from his own peer group and from the rights and obligations associated with his social position as a policeman. The same forces can be said to affect any other community member who shares similar degrees of limited social out-group contact and a specialized in-group system of rewards and sanctions.

The creation and reinforcement of these group processes appear to operate most strongly on two occasions. One is during the assembly period at the beginning of each shift; the other occurs during spontaneous gathering of police officers following an incident of an especially dangerous or emotionally arousing nature.

During the assembly period at the beginning of a shift there is a phenomenon which can best be labelled as a warm-up process. There is consistently an amount of good-natured horseplay and needling which takes place during these sessions which serve as a preliminary to the shift. During this time announcements are made to the patrolmen, the sergeants read off special notices of stolen cars, missing persons, escapees, and wanted subjects. Assignments to special details or to particular vehicles are made, notices of court appearances are passed on, and other official business is taken care of in this fifteen-minute period. The joshing and sharp but good-natured kidding that goes on during these sessions suggest that they also serve a very important psychological function.

Policemen live other roles in their lives as individual human beings, and they are coming from those roles into their police roles for eight hours, despite the fact that technically policemen are on duty twenty-four hours a day. To the extent that police work involves different attitudes and philosophies about life and about one's own behavior than do their other roles, these sessions help in making the transition.

Among the purposes served by these sessions, the following would seem to be included. First, the good humor and mutual needling seems to serve the purpose of group cohesion, since this process communicates to the participants that they are part of the group. One wonders, then, about those few officers who do not participate in these activities and their relationship to the group. It may be that those officers who do not participate would also perform differently in the field than those who do. It is noticeable that there is probably less mutual horseplay between persons who differ in their length of service in the department. Those who are older participate in the warm-up activities less than those who are relatively new to the force.

A second important function of the warm-up is that it serves to discharge tension and hostility in a humorous way. This can be seen as a response to the uncertainty of what the policeman may encounter in the ensuing shift and the very real possibility of encountering violence and hostility. By trying out a kind of oneupmanship with each other during this period, the policemen prepare themselves to face challenging encounters with citizens of the community. Perhaps the discharge of hostility through needling serves to help the officer to keep these impulses under control when he is actually encountering a subject in the course of work.

A parallel phenomenon occurs at the end of a shift or following emotionally charged events such as armed robberies and high-speed chases. This may be termed a *cooling-off* process, but it, too, serves some important psychological functions.

At the termination of a work shift, police officers reassemble informally to turn in citations for the supervisor's approval and to complete and file reports. The level of discussion can best be described as loose, since many of the officers are fatigued, and there are frequent expressions of disgust or amazement at their experiences during the shift. This process is more animated following specific emotionally-laden experiences. The officers exchange their observations of the event and openly express their feelings and opinions about it. Those involved in the event describe their reactions and those not involved directly suggest how they believe they would behave under similar circumstances. The author has described elsewhere (Mann, 1971) how this postcrisis emotional comparison process can be influential in establishing group norms. In general, these cooling-off sessions serve to relieve some of the frustration-induced anger and resentment which the policeman might build up during his shift on duty.

Another important function of the cooling-off session is that it serves to bring the officers back together once more after they have been relatively isolated on patrol during the shift. This serves to renew group ties before going off duty, and to reassert the importance of group membership. Further testimony to the importance of this effect is a monthly party which is held by the members of the evening shift at the time shift assignments change. Since they will be changing to day-time assignments, there is a longer than usual time between work shifts, and this party serves both as a celebration and an affirmation of group spirit.

Another group dynamic influence has been observed in the course of efforts to establish consultation relationships with field supervisors, who hold the rank of sergeant. It was comparatively easy to consult with the supervisory personnel at the level of captain and lieutenant, and with the young patrolmen and cadets. However, repeated difficulty was encountered in attempting to establish contact with the sergeants. In general, they were the least well informed about the purposes of consultation, and efforts to schedule training sessions with them to develop relationships were consistently delayed.

The sergeants appear to be key figures in efforts to help policemen in handling disturbed behavior in the community because of the potential influence they could exert over patrolmen. On the basis of theory and previous research they were not expected to be the most inaccessible group (Mann, 1972), and this phenomenon demanded further study.

In an effort to better understand this problem several key

personnel were interviewed with reference to this occurrence. By and large, the information obtained did not provide answers which were entirely satisfactory. The most frequent response obtained was that there was no real problem except difficulties of scheduling. However, using this information as a starting point, clues to some aspects of this phenomenon may be suggested.

The patrol activities of the police department may be viewed organizationally as one of the most insulated segments of police activity relative to outside innovations. There are real reasons for this state of affairs in the form of relatively little face-to-face contact with peers, maximal spatial dispersion of activities, and a high degree of individual discretion in decision making compared to other police activities. Bittner (1970) has analyzed these factors in detail. As primary supervisors of this activity, the patrol sergeants would seem to exercise considerable relative autonomy within the department.

While it is true that finding free time for scheduling training sessions with these supervisors could be a problem, few people in the department acknowledged that this was a significant factor. It seems more meaningful to view this phenomenon in the dynamic terms of a power-dependency relationship, such as the model suggested by Dalton, Barnes and Zaleznik (1968).

Some interviewees felt that maintenance of control over field supervisors by command level officers (lieutenants and captains) was an important domain of influence. If, as the analysis presented here suggests, this control is tenuous, then it makes sense that its maintenance would be closely guarded. Command level supervisors can ill afford to have their immediate subordinates acquire skills over which they themselves do not feel a sense of mastery, because the legitimacy of their assessments of performance and administration of rewards in this area might be questioned. Since most of the command level supervisors' reward power lies in approval or disapproval of the arrest behavior of the patrols, by determining whether or not a booking will be made, the expansion of subordinates' competencies into areas not under this kind of control can be expected to be viewed with circumspection. It can be hypothesized that this tendency may be exaggerated when the power dependency relationship is based on a limited range of rewards which can only partially influence subordinate behavior.

On the other hand, since the approval or disapproval of arrest behavior is a key factor in the policeman's role as it is typically defined, this aspect of reward structure is a powerful influence over the field supervisors. It is understandable that they may complement the viewpoint of the command supervisors by restricting their own role commitments to behaviors which fall within the domain to which rewards can be applied.

Another factor in the relative inaccessibility of the uniformed sergeants as a group may be a degree of competition between the different shifts, the organizational element with which they are most closely identified. Evaluations of shift performance are made in part on a comparative basis and there is some intershift social comparison which is generated by this process. This state of affairs could serve as a barrier to bringing the field supervisors together as a group, but it is probably of secondary importance to the factors involved in the command-field supervisors relationships.

The failure to anticipate these occurrences was due partly to incomplete understanding of how the theory should be applied to the particulars of the police department. A formal analysis of the organizational structure of the department would suggest that lower ranking personnel should be more accessible to innovation, based on the assumption that lower status is associated with weaker ties to central authority. While it is questionable whether this assumption holds for police organization, a more *functional* analysis of police organization would have highlighted the relative autonomy of the field supervisors and their mutual interdependence with the command level supervisors, which can now be described from hindsight. It is worth noting that this interdependence is heavily supported by the internal police norms about what constitutes proper (rewardable) police behavior.

This analysis of reward structure can contribute more than merely to qualify the limitations on introducing innovations in police work. It can point out why a training program may be difficult to implement, but it can also illuminate why training alone is insufficient and suggest other required modes of change.

In essence, this analysis indicates that in order for a change in police behavior to endure, the resultant changes in role relations must be given official as well as unofficial legitimacy, not merely through public pronouncement, but by establishing a record-keeping system which will reflect the changed behavior and by making provisions for rewarding such behavior within the role of the policeman, rather than in an *ad hoc* fashion, such as through occasional citations of merit. Additionally, both supervisors and consultants could make more deliberate use of the normally occurring social comparison processes to establish changes in mutual expectations and self-evaluations. In turn, such processes could improve supervisory practices and, potentially, overall police effectiveness. This informal kind of in-service training may ultimately be more effective than several varieties of classroom sessions.

It must be recognized that policemen already perform a broad range of activities, only some of which are officially designated as part of the policeman's role. In reality, these tasks are of at least equal importance to the community as those which are publicly recognized. But the enormity of the task of redefining and achieving normative support for changes in role designations cannot be taken lightly. Already this debate has reached the level of several Presidential commissions, and the issues are far from being settled. The point of these remarks is that while social-psychological understanding of police reward structure and the development of innovative techniques are helpful and necessary, the redefinition and recognition of police role functions is a product of social forces larger than a consultation program or a police department. It is properly the result of a community process of debate, goal setting, and decision making, and while one sees all too little of the last two parts of this process on the contemporary scene, increased police competence and appropriate rewards for performance are one means of initiating such a process.

Even within current conditions in most communities, there is enough freedom to change that the observations presented here could be implemented to a degree large enough to be beneficial. It is not being suggested that social-psychological knowledge will solve problems by itself, but competent police administrators are making increasing use of knowledge from this field and others in trying to deal with problems which require all the knowledge which can be brought to bear on them. Further studies of these processes can surely be beneficial. To recall Gardner's (1968) observation, it may be that the hardest part of the task will be to recognize the need.

NOTES

1. Recent findings indicate that policemen do not differ significantly from others of similar socio-economic background in authoritarianism (Niederhoffer, 1967).
2. This view has not been correct at all times in history. See Niederhoffer (1967) and Marx (1970).

8

OBSERVATIONS ON POWER AND AUTHORITY FROM A TRAINING PROGRAM FOR POLICE MANAGERS

FRANKLIN W. NEFF and BERNARD LUBIN

AN acceleration of interest in power and authority issues as they relate to police departments has been shown in recent years. The subject has been approached from various perspectives (Bittner, 1970; Earle, 1972; Wilson, 1968). This chapter will examine some of those issues from a social-psychological perspective and use experiences in a management training program for police managers to illustrate them.[1]

Presented first will be some general views regarding a few of the factors which affect the behavior of police officers and police managers. Then we will examine them in terms of the training program.

The general perspective taken here is that human needs for security, respect, power, and accomplishment interact with societal and organizational values, procedures, and expectations to create distributions of influence and responsibility which are associated with social roles. Any given distribution may be functional or dysfunctional for the attainment of organizational or personal goals at one point in time and not so at another. One aspect of major social change is the redistribution or modification of the relative amounts of influence and responsibility associated with given roles.

The initiation of management training in this police department[2] came about because of the desire to improve decision-making relationships among units and individuals in the department, and relationships with organizations and individuals outside the department.

This wish for improvement was expressed in terms of beliefs that organizational goals could be better attained and individual satisfaction increased by changes in managerial behavior. The changes generally could be understood as involving issues of power and responsibility which are common in organizational life in the United States. Should more people participate in problem solving, especially decision making? Should people in various organizational roles be required to account for their actions to others in equal or lower roles in the hierarchy? To what extent should other forms of influence — for example, reward or expert information — be used instead of coercion among members of the department? Or with outsiders?

As stated above, such issues are common in organizational life in the United States (Dalton, Barnes & Zalenik, 1968; Perrow, 1972). It may be that such issues have added significance when the organization has societal authorization to apply coercive power — ultimately physical force — in performing its functions. While business and industrial organizations may be able to apply large amounts of coercion through the control of economic rewards, they seldom legally can use physical force. Police departments are created to provide for the application of physical force.

In his monograph titled "The Functions of the Police in Modern Society," Bittner (1970) says that the capacity to use force is the core of the police role. He gives a more precise definition when he says, " ... the role of the police is best understood as a mechanism for the distribution of nonnegotiably coercive force employed in accordance with the dictates of an intuitive grasp of situational exigencies" (p. 46). With such a concept of the function of police, it is not difficult to see why there would be high concern for power and authority and their uses by the people who are members of police departments. This function of the application of force is frequently accompanied by a requirement for very rapid decision and action. Such a requirement typically produces authority structures in which influence and responsibility are centralized, relatively permanent, and relatively clearly specified. All three attributes of the power distribution may be sources of organizational dysfunction and individual dissatisfaction, especially when societal viewpoints and values are changing.

With the central function of the police thus being the use, or threat of use, of coercive power, it seems likely that any activities of the police which are viewed as affecting that function will be important to police officers. Such activities will be considered by officers within the framework of their effect on the ability to exercise that coercive power. One would anticipate that officers (or anyone expected to apply coercive power) would want to establish psychological dominance; would prefer simple (rather than complex) definitions of situations; would prefer clear and specific guidelines for action; and would want to be responsible to a single, consistent, authoritative superior. While these implications have been phrased from the viewpoint of the police officer, they infer both individual characteristics and characteristics of the social situation.

There are a number of additional social and psychological factors which influence police behavior around issues of authority and power. Some of these will be discussed here, the social factors first.

Bittner's definition of the role of police was developed from his examination of the work of the police and of the expectations held for them by the public. This is reflected in Bittner's analysis when he writes that many people see the police as an agency which can be used to compel others to do what they want them to do. In a series of very brief vignettes of police activity (Bittner, 1970, pp. 39-40), Bittner makes clear the fact that police are often called to a situation because a citizen wishes the police to use force to compel another party to do what they wish to have done. This kind of public expectation and public demand on the police has a way of either developing role expectations or reinforcing role expectations about their function as employers of force.

In the course of their socialization as police officers, many things happen which develop their conceptions of their role and of the expectations held by citizens and fellow officers. One element of this is the demand for rapid decision under stress.

While managers in many organizations applaud the ability to make good decisions rapidly, this characteristic may be especially desired in organizations such as the police, where violence or the threat of violence is frequently present and to some extent contingent upon the rapid decision making of the officer. These experiences during socialization into the police force have a way of carrying over, so that officers in managerial positions still believe that it is important to make decisions with great speed. It would appear that decisions to be made by police managers, as is the case with managers in other organizations, often have less pressing time requirements than is the case with officers on the beat.

Members of police departments and observers frequently refer to police departments as paramilitary organizations. To some extent, this is an accurate description. Such a view of the police, however, also encourages the application of some of the military stereotypes to the police departments, some of them being: unquestioned obedience, acceptance of the decisions of superiors, and some tendency to see the use of force to make one's decisions stick, or be implemented as appropriate. Officers in the training program reported that these behaviors were exhibited by other officers. Occasionally they exhibited them themselves, but perhaps no more frequently than many people in our society.

An additional social factor influencing police officers in their handling of power in their organizations is common to people working in most organizations. The distribution of authority and responsibility tends to be hierarchical, with more of it at the top and lesser amounts at lower levels. Thus, each level is understood to obtain its authority from, and to be dependent upon, the next higher level. This relatively authoritarian structure is generally characteristic of the organizations in which most people work and of other organizations with which most of us are familiar: recreational, civic, and religious. Police departments are expected to be the same, and those expectations encourage the use of power in authoritarian ways.

When we focus on psychological factors influencing the behavior of police officers relevant to the exercise of power, we find that some research by Rokeach (1970) provides evidence of a preference for authoritarian approaches among some police officers. An extreme form of the exercise of physical coercion by a small number of police officers was discussed by Toch (1969). Toch examined, among other things, police officers who were frequently involved in violence. He found that they were often dealing with concerns about power.

While we did not observe tendencies toward violence among

police officers in our work, we did learn that some people are attracted to police work by a desire to be "where the action is", this seemed to reflect an interest in acting on problems of bringing about a change in a situation in which the exercise of power was an element. An example of this was given by a junior officer who participated in the problem identification sessions prior to the management training program. He described his annoyance at chasing around to different parts of the city to turn off fire hydrants which youngsters had been turning on. He was annoyed because, while he was forced to deal with what he considered an inconsequential matter, the rest of the police force were dealing with a major conflict.

Some of the other social-psychological factors are discussed by Kirkham (1975). He points out that officers, especially those on beats in high poverty areas, are subjected to intense and repeated threats to their safety and self-esteem. Such conditions appear to rapidly escalate a need to demonstate power and dominance and to develop a view of others as inferior.

Thus, the psychological characteristics apparently nurtured and reinforced in police work reflect an authoritarian, hierarchical approach to power and authority issues.

An additional dimension is added when one considers the fact that some major changes in values and in power relations appear to be under way in many aspects of American society. At about the same time Bittner was developing his statement, Earle (1972) was completing his report of a study of authoritarian versus nonauthoritarian training of police enforcement officers in Los Angeles County. Earle states that there appear to be changes moving throughout our society in directions which reduce acceptance of authoritarian approaches. In the final chapter of his report, he points to changes being made in the military, including West Point and the Officer Candidate School at Ft. Benning, Georgia. These changes are in the direction of the reduction of the more authoritarian approaches. Earle further argues that these changes are a considered response to changes in American society which he suggests is less receptive to authoritarian views and more concerned with the growth and development of the individual (Earle, 1972). (A further discussion of these issues can be found in Bennis,

1973.) Given the analysis of Bittner and the point of view argued by Earle, it would not be surprising that police officers find themselves in conflict regarding authoritarian approaches to the exercise of power and authority.

To sum up briefly what has been said thus far, it would appear that many factors are operative in the background experiences and the cultural context in which police officers move toward managerial positions. These factors tend to dispose police officers toward the exercise of power and authority, and, to some extent, the exercise of these in a relatively authoritative, if not authoritarian fashion.

As one examines the literature regarding managerial styles and desired managerial behavior in other organizations than the police, it becomes clear that there is no commonly agreed upon managerial style which is seen by scholars and practitioners alike as the more desirable or the more effective style (Stogdill, 1974). Much has been written about the desirability of a manager being a strong leader; much has also been written about the desirability of a manager involving himself in consultation and/or participation with his subordinates and peers in working out decisions and policies. Fielder has developed a theory of contingency leadership (Fielder, 1974) which suggests that the general preferences of the manager, the expectations of the people he is managing, the nature of the task, and the conditions of the environment of the organization are all contingencies affecting a determination of what kinds of leader behavior are most likely to be effective. Reviews of research and other literature regarding leader behavior and management (Current Perspectives in Leadership, 1974) do suggest that flexibility and adaptability on the part of managers may be important requisites. Ability to read the requirements of the situation, to determine one's relationship with subordinates, and to determine the requirements of the environment may be important skills for a manager to have in order to be a successful leader. Reliance on existing distributions of power and authority in organizations may be, if regularly followed, an inappropriate course to take. Although there are times when such an approach to leadership and management may be effective, it seems evident that many times such an approach is not appropriate.

Having taken a relatively generalized view of conditions which influence police officers in approaching management of police departments, we will now identify relevant elements in the situation in which a management training activity program was developed. For several years top management in the department had provided many members with opportunities to give input at the highest levels in the department. While initially not extensive, there was nonetheless encouragement for officers from various parts of the department to report their views and generate information. A particularly important development was the utilization of task forces in analyzing certain issues and making proposals of alternative ways of working with those issues. This task force approach resulted in a number of officers (who were younger and who had differing educational experiences) giving important input toward the future activity plans of the department. One of the consequences of the work of these task forces was a recommendation that managerial training be provided for officers in the department. That report particularly suggested that such management training be extended to the top levels of the department.

A series of meetings involving officers at all levels of the department (above the patrolman level) produced a set of recommendations. From these recommendations, a series of training goals were developed by consultatnts. The consultants also developed a proposal for training which was submitted to the command staff of the department. The command staff and the chief accepted this proposal. Goals which were established for training outcomes included skill development in:

1. Utilizing problem-solving procedures;
2. Defining tasks and specifying what the task requires for oneself and for others;
3. Communicating one's own preferences, needs, directions, and information relevant to organizational works;
4. Obtaining and using information about feelings, both one's own and those of others, as data for problem solving;
5. Problem solving, including ability to perform many of the activities or functions required;
6. Working with conflict of various kinds — between members

of a group, between groups, and between individual and organizational needs;

7. Relating one's unit to the larger organization through communicating about the activities and needs of one's unit in the organization, and communicating about the activities and needs of the organization to one's unit;

8. Relating the Police Department to its environment through communicating the goals and activities and needs of the Police Department to the community, and communicating the responses, needs, and changes in the environment back to the Department.

As these goals indicate, and as the training program to be described below also suggests, the orientation of the training was toward greater officer involvement in managerial policy making and a greater understanding of the impact of their actions on each other. While power equalization was not set as a goal, nor defined as desirable in the training, nonetheless, the general orientation of this training program had implications for the distribution of power and authority.

Turning now to the design and content of the training activities, the orientation from which the trainers worked favored experiential learning (Bradford, Gibb & Benne, 1964). Learning activities were designed in which the officers would have opportunities to experience and together to examine problems of the kind which had been identified by the conferences with officers the preceding year. These training activities frequently took the form of role-playing. There were also many activities which required officers to talk with each other about various problems, to try to analyze these problems, and to consider ways in which alternatives might be generated. A general outline of training activities is provided in Table I.

Next, we would like to consider some of the reactions of some police officers to the training activities in the context of the issues involved in power and authority in management training. One of the activities on the first day of training was the utilization of an experience which permits some comparison of the effects of one-way communication with two-way communication. The activity is set up around a participant describing geometric forms to his

TABLE 8.1

TRAINING TOPICS AND ACTIVITIES

Topic	Activity
Group decision-making	Consensus development around predictions of sergeant and captain preferences for leader behavior.
Leadership styles	Review of leader behavior exhibited by officers in the training activities using categories of differential group participation; also, R. Wallen categories: tough battler, friendly helper, objective thinker.
Communication	One-way, two-way communication exercise to emphasize effects of each.
Problem-solving	Situation-Target-Proposal (S-T-P) approach to problem-solving explained and tried by individuals.
Impact of role and situation on perception and inference	Film: *Eye of the Beholder.*
Group decision-making: use of resources	NASA problem; Coal Company problem. Officers participate or observe; then discuss factors affecting problem-solving.
Management theory	Presentation of Maslow, McGregor, Argyrus.
Group decision-making: leader as facilitator	New car (truck) problem. Officers participate or observe a partly structured group decision-making problem.
Group decision-making: work under stress conditions	Mine Field exercise. Officers simulate group trying to get through a mine field. Activities analyzed for organization established, decisions, reactions.
Evaluation	Evaluation interview role play; officers act as superiors or subordinates

Topic	Activity
	in a discussion of performance.
Group problem-solving: difference in goals	Role play problem involving Community Relations Unit and area patrol unit.
Individual in relationship to organization	Presentation, discussion of *Principles of Organizations Operations.*
Impact of status on group problem-solving	Role play with difference status officers arriving late.
Barriers to change in the Department	Force field analysis; discussions of factors supporting and blocking Police Department change.
Cooperation/competition between units	Planners/operators exercise.
Conflict between units	Role play, Problems Between Units (Tactical and Patrol). Officers participate in or observe problem-solving meeting. Work in "meeting" is analyzed. Conceptual presentation regarding conflict.
Vertical communication regarding policy decisions	Officers identify top-level decisions of importance and concern to lower level managers.
	List the decisions in order of priority, selecting the five most important.
	Describe how those decisions were understood, interpreted, and reacted to by personnel at various levels.
	Formulate questions regarding the decisions.
	Top management discusses decisions.
	Implications for communication and decision-making at various levels of management.
Conflict management	Role play of manager working on conflict between two subordinate units.
Relating to groups out-	Officers divided into two groups, one

Topic	Activity
side the Department	to represent Police Department officers, the other to represent community leaders.
	Each group met separately to formulate requirements for possible Police-Citizen Incident Review Board.
	Each group listed things which interfere with working with the other group.
	Lists were shared and clarified.
	Groups met separately for possible reformulation of requirements.
	Representatives of each group met together to discuss possible Police-Citizen Incident Review Board.
	Exercise analyzed.
Allocation of police cars	Presentation of S-T-P analysis of how cars were currently distributed.
	Discussion of criteria for allocation.

fellows without their seeing them. They are to construct it from his description. The first exercise simply involves the participant delineating it verbally without receiving any response. In the second approach he describes a different pattern, but this time the other participants can ask questions about it (Nylen, Mitchell & Stout, 1967). The officers worked with the activity in ways similar to managers in other organizations. Some problems and frustrations were experienced in both ways of communicating, but the generally superior understanding and execution of the task resulting from two-way communication was noted. After that discussion, one of the trainers asked what the relationship of the experience was to the work of the police officers in the department. One of the most senior officers present responded, "Not a Goddam bit." This response is thought provoking when one considers that some of the problems identified by members of the department in the pretraining phase were the lack of understanding of policy, the lack of input from subordinates in regard to policy statements, and the lack of opportunity to respond to communications emanating from higher levels in the organization.

Another incident occurring later in training tended to emphasize the problems of one-way communication. In that meeting, the top officers below the Chief were meeting with the next echelon below them to review some of the major problems experienced by managers during the previous year. There was considerable discussion about a decision made to allow officers to apply for the qualifying tests for advancement. The decision changed general policy regarding this. In the course of this discussion, it became clear that the lower-ranked officers in these upper levels of management felt quite strongly that their superiors had not listened to their point of view nor involved them in the decisions. The consequence was that they felt that their positions with their subordinates had been weakened. Given this evidence of the negative impact of one-way communication and the need for two-way communication, it was particularly striking, then, that a senior officer would state that there was no relationship between the one-way/two-way communication exercise and problems in the department. It was also instructive that there was very little discussion subsequent to his statement. And certainly none of the other officers challenged his statement.

These events reflect tendencies to accept authority from above as legitimate and to believe that open disagreement with superiors is risky.

Another training activity that was handled interestingly by the police officers also suggests some of the difficulties in examining alternative approaches to the issues around power and authority. This exercise is one developed by N. R. F. Maier which deals with decisions about which members of a team of workers will be the one to receive a new truck (Maier, Solem & Maier, 1957). Maier built this problem around people working for a public utility, specifically a telephone company. The problem is based on each of the members having a vehicle with different age, condition, and operating characteristics. The problem is designed so that the supervisor of the work unit encourages the men to decide among themselves who will receive the new truck. For the purposes of this training activity, the problem was translated to a police department with the group of men being a police patrol unit under one sergeant. The officers, in working through this problem, seemed to have difficulty dealing with a sergeant who tried to facilitate decision making rather than directing the decision making or making the decision himself. Some of the officers commented that the learning activity was unrealistic because a sergeant would never take that posture with his men.

Related to the exercise of power and the use of authority are problems arising from differential status. One of the training activities provided opportunities to look at the difference in responses to comments, ideas, and suggestions of officers of low status as compared to those from officers of high status. One of the officers who participated in a role play as part of this training activity was cast in the role of a sergeant, although he did not know the status level of the role that he was to play. When he came into the role-playing situation and began to interact, he behaved as he would typically behave, as if these were his peers. In very short order, other officers in the role-playing activity communicated to him his status (although the role-playing had been designed so that first names would be used rather than job titles such as sergeant or captain). They evidently felt it important to communicate to this person in the sergeant role that his status was lower than his behavior suggested. Interestingly enough, the officer, (who was in fact a major) whose role in the role-playing game was that of a sergeant, changed his behavior instantly—that is, he exercised much less initiative and tended to listen much more. In the analysis of this activity, the other officers found it very difficult to examine the changes in his behavior and to associate it with differences in status. It was also difficult for them to consider the impact of these status differences on the utilization of available knowledge and ideas for problem solving. This suggests that the idea of reducing power differences will not be easily implemented when it contravenes the existing power structure.

Given the difficulties which the above anecdotes reflect, it is encouraging that the training program did have a favorable impact on the officers. An evaluation of the program (Neff, Lubin, &

McConnell, 1975) found that self-reports of managerial behavior changed in a positive direction from just prior to the training to about three months after it was completed.

To bring about changes in managerial behavior which involve major shifts in power and responsibility in any large organization is not easy. Frequently, reports of success in such training note that one or more of the people in top authority positions permit and encourage overt consideration of such changes by their own changes in behavior, changes which legitimate different, more influential behavior on the part of subordinates (Alschuler, 1972; Bartlett, 1967; Blake, Mouton, Barnes, & Greiner, 1964).

It is important to record that a substantial influence for such changes as did occur in managerial behavior in the department was the Chief's encouragement of activities which permitted and required junior officers to participate in problem solving. A particularly striking example of his encouragement was provided by his acceptance of a training activity which encouraged the officers participating in the training program to review policies of the previous year in a conference setting. This training activity involved the officers in selecting about five of the top level decisions which concerned lower level managers. These were discussed in terms of the impact on lower levels and included questions which the managers had about those decisions. The Chief participated in the conference, responding to questions and providing information about factors affecting the decision. Such openness to questions and willingness to provide information reflected receptivity to influence, and are believed to have facilitated increased power by members of the department over the work and policies of the department.

Also, we wish to take issue with a tendency that we have noticed among some writers to depict police departments as unchanging, thoughtless, monolithic structures managed by system-selected "supercops" with limited potential or vision. To the contrary, our experience and conceptualization suggest that management manpower in police departments shows a wide range of abilities, comparable to those found in other service organizations and in business and industry.

Our overall impressions bear some resemblance to the views of

Kirkham (1975) and Fodor (1975) that one must look to situational factors as well as personality factors for the explanation of police managerial behavior.

NOTES

1. The authors wish to thank Alice Lubin for her stimulation of this chapter and her perceptive reactions to early drafts.
2. The police department referred to is in a large metropolitan city in the midwest. Further information can be found in the article by Neff, Lubin, and McConnell, 1975.

REFERENCES

Alschuler, A.: Toward a self-renewing school. *Journal of Applied Behavioral Science.* 8:577-600, 1972.

Bartlett, A. C.: Changing behavior as a means to increased efficiency. *Journal of Applied Behavioral Science.* 3:381-403, 1967.

Bennis, W. F.: *Beyond Bureaucracy.* New York, McGraw-Hill, 1973.

Bittner, E.: *The functions of the police in modern society.* Washington, D. C., Public Health Service Publication 2059, 1970.

Blake, R. R., Mouton, J. S., Barnes, L. B., and Greiner, L. E.: Breakthrough in organization development. *Harvard Business Review.* 42:133, 1964.

Bradford, L., Gibb, J. R., and Benne, K. D.: *T-group Theory and Laboratory Method.* New York, John Wiley & Sons, 1964.

Current perspectives in leadership. *Journal of Contemporary Business.* 3, 1974.

Dalton, G. W., Barnes, L. B., and Zaleznik, A.: *The Distribution of Authority in Formal Organizations.* Cambridge, The MIT Press, 1968.

Earle, H. H.: An investigation of authoritarian versus nonauthoritarian training in the selection and training of law enforcement officers. *Dissertation Abstracts International.* 33-2a:8090, 1973.

Fiedler, F. E.: The contingency model — new directions for leadership utilization. *Journal of Contemporary Business.* 3:65-80, 1974.

Fodor, E. M.: Authoritarian leadership styles as a function of group stress. Paper presented at Annual Meetings of the American Psychological Association, Chicago, August 30-September 3, 1975.

Kirkham, D. L. Doc cop.: *Human Behavior.* 1974 (May), pp. 17-23.

Maier, N. R. F., Solem, A. R., and Maier, A. A.: *Supervisory and Executive Development; A Manual for Role Playing.* New York, John Wiley & Sons, 1957.

Neff, F. W., Lubin, B., and McConnell, K.: Impact of training on self-description and co-worker description of police managerial behavior.

American Journal of Community Psychology. 3:391-402, 1975.

Nylen, D., Mitchell, J. R., and Stout, A.: *Handbook of Staff Development and Human Relations Training.* Washington, National Training Laboratories Learning Resources Corporation, 1967.

Perrow, C.: *Complex Organizations. A Critical Essay.* Glenview, Scott, Foresman & Co., 1972.

Rokeach, M., Miller, M. G., and Snyder, J. A.: The value gap between police and policed. *Journal of Social Issues.* 27:155-171, 1970.

Stogdill, R. M.: Historical trends in leadership theory and research. *Journal of Contemporary Business.* 3:1-17, 1974.

Toch, H.: *Violent Men.* Chicago, Aldine Publishing Co., 1969.

Wilson, J. Q.: Dilemmas of police administration. *Public Administration Review.* 38:407-417, 1968.

9

THE POLICE IN PROTEST*

National Commission on the Causes and Prevention
of Violence   (A Staff Report)

THE POLICE AND MASS PROTEST:
THE ESCALATION OF CONFLICT
HOSTILITY AND VIOLENCE

O NE central fact emerges from any study of police encounters with student protesters, anti-war demonstrators or black militants; there has been a steady escalation of conflict, hostility and violence.

The Black Community

Writing in 1962 three years before the Watts riots and almost the distant past in this respect, James Baldwin vividly portrayed the social isolation of the policeman in the black ghetto:

> ... The only way to police a ghetto is to be oppressive. None of the Police Commissioner's men, even with the best will in the world, have any way of understanding the lives led by the people; they swagger about in twos and threes patrolling. Their very presence is an insult, and it would be, even if they spent their entire day feeding gumdrops to children. They represent the force of the white world, and that world's real intentions are, simply, for that world's criminal profit and ease, to keep the black man corralled up here, in his place. The badge, the gun in the holster, and the swinging club, make vivid what will happen should his rebellion become overt ...
>
> It is hard, on the other hand, to blame the policeman, blank, goodnatured, thoughtless, and insuperably innocent, for being such a perfect representative of the people he serves. He, too, believes in good intentions and is astounded and offended when they are not taken for the deed. He has never, himself, done

---

*Reprinted from U.S. Government publication: *The Politics of Protest*, Chapter 7, 1969.

anything for which to be hated — which of us has? And yet he is facing, daily and nightly, the people who would gladly see him dead, and he knows it. There is no way for him not to know it: There are few things under heaven more unnerving than the silent, accumulating contempt and hatred of a people. He moves through Harlem, therefore, like an occupying soldier in a bitterly hostile country; which is precisely what, and where he is, and is the reason he walks in twos and threes.[1]

Today the situation is even more polarized. There have been riots, and both black Americans and police have been killed. Black anger has become more and more focused on the police: the Watts battle cry of "Get Whitey" has been replaced by the Black Panther slogan: "Off the pigs." The black community is virtually unanimous in demanding major reforms, including police review boards and local control of the police. According to the Kerner Commission[2] and other studies,[3] conflict with the police was one of the most important factors in producing black riots. In short, anger, hatred and fear of the police are a major common denominator among black Americans at the present time.

The police return these sentiments in kind — they both fear the black community and openly express violent hostility and prejudice toward it. Our review of studies of the police revealed unanimity in findings on this point: the majority of rank and file policemen are hostile toward black people.[4] Usually such hostility does not reflect official policy, although in isolated instances, as in the Miami Police Department under Chief Headley, official policy may encourage anti-black actions.[5] Judging from these studies, there is no reason to suppose that anti-black hostility is a new development brought on by recent conflicts between the police and the black community. What appears to have changed is not police attitudes, but the fact that black people are fighting back.

The Harlem Riot Commission Report of 1935 reserved its most severe criticism for the police:

> The police of Harlem show too little regard for human rights and constantly violate their fundamental rights as citizens ...
> The insecurity of the individual in Harlem against police aggression is one of the most potent causes for the existing hostility to authority ... It is clearly the responsibility of the police to act in such a way as to win the confidence of the citizens of

Harlem and to prove themselves the guardians of the rights and safety of the community rather than its enemies and oppressors.[6]

And William A. Westley reported from his studies of police in the late forties:

No white policeman with whom the author has had contact failed to mock the Negro, to use some type of stereotyped categorization, and to refer to interaction with the Negro in an exaggerated dialect, when the subject arose.[7]

Students of police seem unanimous in agreeing that police attitudes have not changed much since those studies. In a study done under a grant from the Office of Law Enforcement Assistance of the United States Department of Justice, and submitted to the President's Commission on Law Enforcement and the Administration of Criminal Justice in 1966, Donald J. Black and Albert J. Reiss, Jr. found overwhelming evidence of widespread, virulent prejudice by police against Negroes.[8] Their study was based on field observations by thirty-six observers who accompanied police officers for a period of seven weeks in the summer of 1966 in Boston, Chicago, and Washington, D. C. It was found that 38 percent of the officers had expressed "extreme prejudice," while an additional 34 percent had expressed "considerable prejudice" in front of the observers. Thus, 72 percent of these policemen qualified as prejudiced against black Americans. It must be remembered that these views were not solicited, but were merely recorded when voluntarily expressed. And it seems fair to assume that some proportion of the remaining 28 percent were sophisticated enough to exercise a certain measure of restraint when in the presence of the observers. Also, examples presented by Black and Reiss make it clear that their observers found intense and bitter hatred toward blacks. Moreover, these are not rural southern policemen, and our investigation has shown that their views are typical of those in most urban police forces.

Concrete examples of this prejudice are not hard to find. For example, the Commission's Cleveland Study Team found that prejudice had been festering in the Cleveland police force for a long time but suddenly bloomed into virulent bigotry following the July, 1968 shootout between police and black militants. While white police were withdrawn from the ghetto for one night to allow black community leaders to quell the rioting, racist abuse of Mayor Carl B. Stokes, a Negro, could be heard on the police radio. And posters with a picture of the Mayor under the words "WANTED FOR MURDER" hung in district stations for several weeks after the shoot-out. Elsewhere our interviews disclosed the fact that nightsticks and riot batons are at times referred to as "nigger knockers."[9] Robert Conot writes that "LSMFT — the old Lucky Strike slogan — has slipped into police argot as: "Let's Shoot a Mother-Fucker Tonight."[10]

Police actions often reflect these attitudes. In recent years there have been numerous allegations by Negro and civil liberties groups of police insulting, abusing, mistreating, and even beating or murdering blacks. Studies of the police by independent bodies tend to support these allegations. For instance, the 1961 report on *Justice* of the United States Civil Rights Commission concluded that "Police brutality ... is a serious problem in the United States."[11] Without presently recounting specific additional instances and varieties of misconduct, suffice it to say that this conclusion finds support throughout the literature on police.[12]

The problem has become even more acute with the emergence of increased black militancy. Reports in numerous cities, including Detroit,[13] San Francisco,[14] New York,[15] and Oakland,[16] indicate that police officers have attacked or shot members of the black community, often Black Panthers, at offices, social events, and even court house halls. Indeed, it appears that such incidents are spreading and are not isolated in a few police departments.

Moreover, difficult to document, it seems clear that police prejudice impairs the capacity of the police to engage in impartial crowd control. If anything, the behavior which typifies day-to-day policing is magnified in riot situations. The report of the Kerner Commission indicates that, for example, police violence was out of control during the 1967 riots,[17] and similar findings are seen elsewhere,[18] including the study of the Commission's Cleveland Study Team.

Protesters: Student and Anti-War

Conflict has not only been escalating between the police and the black community; bad feeling and violence between the police and students and peace groups has also increased.

The earliest peace marches were treated much like ordinary parades by the police, and the protesters, many of whom accepted nonviolence as their guiding principle, seldom baited the police or expressed hostility toward them. But slowly incidents began accumulating until by the spring and summer of 1968 protest marches frequently became clashes between protesters and the police.

As discussed in our chapter on anti-war protest, the escalation of the war led to growing frustrations and greater militancy on the part of protesters. Yet the police handling of protesters was often unrestrained and only increased the potential for violence — in the immediate situation and for the future. Predictably, the escalation continued. Protesters grew bitterly angry; and as anger against the police became a major element in protest meetings and marches, the police grew to hate and fear the protesters even more. Numerous respected commissions, among them the Cox Commission,[19] which studied the student uprising at Columbia University, and the Sparling Commission,[20] which studied the April, 1968 peace march in Chicago, found that the police used uncalled-for force, often vindictively, against protesters, often regardless of whether the latter were "peaceful" or "provocative."

The extent of violence in police-protester confrontations was most clearly shown to the nation by the media coverage of the 1968 Democratic National Convention in Chicago. What was shown and reported confirmed what some people already thought, confused others, but probably changed few minds. However, the investigation of this Commission's Chicago Study Team documents "unrestrained and indiscriminate police violence on many occasions."

> During the week of the Democratic National Convention, the Chicago police were the targets of mounting provocation by both word and act. It took the form of obscene epithets, and of rocks, sticks, bathroom tiles and even human feces hurled at police by demonstrators. Some of these acts had been planned; others were spontaneous or were themselves provoked by police action. Furthermore, the police had been put on edge by widely

published threats of attempts to disrupt both the city and the Convention.

That was the nature of the provocation. The nature of the response was unrestrained and indiscriminate police violence on many occasions, particularly at night.

That violence was made all the more shocking by the fact that it was often inflicted upon persons who had broken no law, disobeyed no order, made no threat. These included peaceful demonstrators, onlookers, and large numbers of residents who were simply passing through, or happened to live in, the areas where confrontations were occurring.

Newsmen and photographers were singled out for assault, and their equipment deliberately damaged. Fundamental police training was ignored; and officers, when on the scene, were often unable to control their men. As one police officer put it: "What happened didn't have anything to do with police work."[21]

Significantly, the violent police actions seen on television were less fierce than the brutality they displayed at times or places where there were no television cameras present.[22]

What is truly unique about Chicago, however, is not the occurrence of police violence; rather, it is the extent and quality of media coverage given to the actual events, the fact that a respected commission with sufficient resources chose to find out what happened, and the extent and quality of media coverage of the report on those findings. For similar violence has occurred in many places, including New York, San Francisco, and Los Angeles.

For example, in March, 1968, in New York's Grand Central Station, while demonstrators engaged in typical Yippie tactics, police suddenly appeared and, without giving the crowd any real chance to disperse, indiscriminately attacked and clubbed demonstrators.[23] A similar outburst occurred a month later in Washington Square,[24] and of course the police violence that spring at Columbia is by now a matter of common knowledge. The dispersal of a march of thousands to Century City in Los Angeles during the summer of 1967 is also a case in point. There, as reported in *Day of Protest, Night of Violence,* a report prepared by the American Civil Liberties Union of Southern California, dispersal was accompanied by similar police clubbing and beating of demonstrators, children, and invalids.[25] It should be emphasized that the decision to disperse that march was at best questionable since the protesters were not a violent, threatening crowd. Moreover, the report finds that the paraders did not violate the terms of their parade permit, and thus "the order to disperse was arbitrary, and served no lawful purpose."[26]

The point that the Chicago Convention violence is not unique is highlighted by considering that in April, 1968, four months earlier, similar violence occurred between police and protesters during another peace march in Chicago. An investigation was conducted by an independent committee which was chaired by Dr. Edward J. Sparling, president emeritus of Roosevelt University, and whose membership included such persons as Professor Harry Kalven, Jr., of the Chicago Law School and Mr. Warren Bacon, vice president of the Inland Steel Corporation. To quote from the report of this committee:

> On April 27, at the peace parade of the Chicago Peace Council, the police badly mishandled their task. Brutalizing demonstrators without provocation, they failed to live up to that difficult professionalism which we demand.
>
> Yet to place primary blame on the police would, in our view, be inappropriate. The April 27 stage had been prepared by the Mayor's designated officials weeks before. Administrative actions concerning the April 27 Parade were designed by City Officials to communicate that "these people have no right to demonstrate or express their views." Many acts of brutal police treatment on April 27 were directly observed (if not commanded) by the Superintendent of Police or his deputies.[27]

What happened during the Chicago Convention, therefore, is not something totally different from police work *in practice.* Our analysis indicates that the Convention violence was unusual more in the fact of its having been documented than in the fact of its having occurred. The problem most definitely is not one unfortunate outburst of misbehavior on the part of a few officers, as the report of the Chicago Administration alleged.[28]

In closing this section, it is instructive to note two facts; first, that the behavior of most police, most of the time, is not necessarily represented by their actions in situations involving protest.

In protest situations their own political views often seem to control their actions. Secondly, a violent response by police to protesters is not inevitable. For example, recently a major London demonstration protesting the Vietnam war and the politics of the "Establishment" resulted in no serious violence, and one serious attempt to provoke trouble was avoided by a superbly disciplined and restrained team of policemen. According to *The New York Times*:

> ... But the police never drew their truncheons and never showed anger. They held their line in front of the embassy until, as the attackers tired, they could begin to push the crowd down South Audley Street and away from the square.
>
> Americans who saw the Grosvenor Square events could not help drawing the contrast with the violence that erupted between the Chicago police and demonstrators at the Democratic Convention in August.[29]

More recently, in the United States, during the inaugural ceremonies for President Nixon, the Washington, D. C. authorities and city police received a complimentary reaction from all sides. David Dellinger called the police performance "beautiful" and added that, "At key points the Mayor and other people stepped in to prevent [violence] from escalating." The *Washington Daily News*, in an editorial of January 22, 1969, described the conduct of the police as "a superb demonstration of discipline — a new, professional police force awesome in its strength and self-control." In the materials that follow, we shall attempt to analyze those features of the policeman's role in society that contribute to a breakdown of discipline and self-control.

The Predicament of the Police

The significance of police hostility, anger and violence need hardly be stressed. Yet any analysis along this line runs the risk of being labelled antipolice, an it is often argued that such analyses demand more of the police than of other groups in society. However, this criticism may both be true and miss the point.

In some senses we do demand more of the police than we do of other groups — or more accurately, perhaps, we become especially concerned when the police fail to meet our demands. But this *must* be the case because it is to the police that we look to deal with so many of our problems and it is to the police that we entrust the legitimate use of force. Moreover, unnecessary police violence can only exacerbate the problems police action is used to solve. Protesters are inflamed, and a cycle of greater and greater violence is set into motion — both in the particular incident and in future incidents. More fundamentally, the misuse of police force violates basic notions of our society concerning the role of police. Police are not supposed to adjudicate and punish; they are supposed to apprehend and take into custody. To the extent to which a nation's police step outside such bounds, that nation has given up the role of law in a self-defeating quest for order.

So it becomes especially important to explore *why* the police have become increasingly angry and hostile toward blacks and protesters and why they are inclined to overreact violently when confronting such persons. The necessary starting point is a careful examination of what it is like to be a policeman today.

The predicament of the police in America today can scarcely be overstated, caught as they are between two contradictory developments: their job is rapidly becoming much more difficult (some say impossible), while at the same time their resources — morale, material and training — are deteriorating. No recent observer doubts that the police are under increasing strain largely because they are increasingly being given tasks well beyond their resources.

The Policeman's Job

The outlines of the growing demands upon the police are well known and require but brief review here. Increasingly, the police are required to cope with the problems which develop as conditions in the black community remain intolerable and as black anger and frustration grow. Yet all intelligent police observers recognize that the root causes of black violence and rebellion are beyond the means or authority of the police. As former Superintendent of the Chicago Police Department, O. W. Wilson, commented on riots in a recent interview:

> I think there is a long-range answer — the correction of the
> inequities we're all aware of: higher educational standards, im-
> proved economic opportunities, a catching up on the cultural
> lag, a strengthening of spiritual values. All of these things in the
> long run must be brought to bear on the problem if it is to be
> solved permanently, and obviously it must be solved. It will be
> solved, but not overnight.[30]

Since the publication of the Kerner Commission Report there is
no longer much reason for anyone not to understand the nature of
the social ills underlying the symptomatic violence of the black
ghettos. But while we all know what needs to be done, it has not
been done. The American policeman as well as the black American must therefore suffer daily from the consequence of inaction
and indifference.

James Bladwin's characterization of the police as an army of
occupation, quoted earlier, requires more and more urgent consideration. The police are set against the hatred and violence of
the ghetto and are delegated to suppress it and keep it from
seeping into white areas. Significantly, no one knows this better
than the police who must try to perform this dangerous and increasingly unmanageable and thankless task. Throughout our
interviews with members of major urban police forces, their de-
spair and anger in the face of worsening violence and impending
disaster was evident. No recent account about the police by
scholars and journalists reports evidence to the contrary. As the
Saturday Evening Post recently wrote of the police in St. Louis:
"To many policemen, the very existence of [an emergency riot
mobilization] plan implies that it will be used, and it is this sense
of inevitability, this feeling that events have somehow slipped out
of their control, that unnerves and frustrates them ...."[31]

And, of course, the police are correct. Events are slipping out of
their control and they must live, more than most people, with the
threat of danger and disaster. As one patrolman told a *Post* reporter, "the first guys there [responding to the riot plan] —
they've had it. I've thought of getting myself a little sign saying
'expendable' and hanging it around my neck."[32] When the tem-
peratures rise about 100 degrees in the ghetto and tenements
overrun with people, rats, hopelessness and anger, it is the police

who are on the line; and any mistake can bring death. A New York policeman interviewed by our Task Force put the widespread apprehensions of the police simply: "Yeah, I'm scared. All the cops are. You never know what's going to happen out there. This place is a powder keg. You don't know if just putting your hand on a colored kid will cause a riot."

Similarly, the police can do little to ameliorate the reasons for student and political protest. Many demands of the protesters — moral political leadership, peace, and reform of the universities — lie outside the jurisdiction of the police. But when protesters are met with police, protest becomes a problem for the police.

Protest, moreover, poses an *unusual* problem for the policeman. Although policemen are characteristically referred to as law-enforcement officers, more than one student of police has distinguished between the patrolman's role as a "peace officer" concerned with public order,[33] and the policeman's role as detective, concerned with enforcing the law. As a peace officer, the patrolman usually copes with his responsibilities by looking away from minor thefts, drunkenness, disturbances, assaults, and malicious mischief. "[T]he normal tendency of the police," writes James Q. Wilson, "is to underenforce the law."[34]

In protest situations, however, the police are in the public eye, and frequently find themselves in the impossible position of acting as substitutes for necessary political and social reform. If they cope with their situation by venting their rage on the most apparent and available source of their predicament — blacks, students and demonstrators — it should occasion no surprise. The professional restraint, compassion and detachment, oftentimes displayed by police, are admirable. Under pressure and provocation, however, the police themselves can pose serious social problems.

The Resources of the Police

As the job of the policeman has become more important and sensitive, society has neglected the police in quite direct ways. From our study of the police in many cities it is apparent that law enforcement as an occupation has declined badly.

The Problem of Manpower: Quantity and Quality

It is hard to say why men join the police force, but the evidence we have indicates that police recruits are not especially sadistic or even authoritarian, as some have alleged. On the contrary, the best evidence that we have been able to accumulate from the works of such police experts as Niederhoffer[35] and MacNamara[36] suggests that the policeman is usually an able and gregarious young man with social ideals, better than average physical prowess and a rather conventional outlook on life, including normal aspirations and self-interest.

One outstanding problem of the police is a decline in pay relative to comparable occupations.[37] Correspondingly, the prestige of the occupation in the estimate of the general public has fallen sharply, and there has been a sharp decline in the quality and quantity of new recruits.[38] Most departments have many vacancies. In New York City, for example, according to a study conducted by Arthur Niederhoffer,[39] more than half of the recruits to the New York City Police in June, 1940, were college graduates. During the last decade, on the other hand, the proportion of recruits with a college degree has rarely reached 5 percent. Niederhoffer attributes this change to a decline in the relative financial rewards for being a policeman.[40] He notes that: "In the 1930's ... top-grade patrolmen in New York City earned three thousand dollars a year. They owned houses and automobiles; they could afford the luxuries that were the envy of the middle class; and they were never laid off. In the panic of the Depression, the middle class began to regard a police career pragmatically."[41] However, as the affluence of the country has risen in general, the relative rewards of police work have lagged badly. "Patrolmen's pay in major cities now averages about $7,500 per year — 33 percent less than is needed to sustain a family of four in moderate circumstances in a large city, according to the U. S. Bureau of Labor Statistics."[42] Even though a top-grade patrolman in New York now earns about $9,000, this is less than a skilled craft-worker, such as an electrician or plumber, earns in New York.[43] Meanwhile, we have encouraged police to aspire to a middle-class lifestyle. To achieve this, many police "moonlight" on a second job and have wives who work. Others — we do not know what percentage — engage in graft and corruption, which, in some cities, has been described as "a way of life."[44]

Thus a decline in the relative salary of the police profession is at least partly to blame for the fact that, while we have increasingly become committed to professionalism among the police, in many of our great cities the quality of recruits has actually been declining. In fact, matters are worse than they might appear; for while the average level of education among police recruits has been declining, the average level of educational achievement in the population has been increasing rapidly. Thus, new police recruits are being taken from an ever-shrinking pool of undereducated persons; increasingly it is such people who find being a policeman a "good job."[45]

In many urban departments today the older policemen are better educated and qualified than are the young policemen — a reversal of the trend operating in almost every other occupation in America. As an Oakland police captain with twenty-seven years on the force described changes in his department to our interviewer:

> We are not getting the type of college people in the department that we were before. The guys that we're getting now have had a high school education, have gone into the army for a couple of years and have come out and are looking to get in the police department because of the good pay. Oakland is a relatively high-paying department, but still does not get educated recruits. We're not getting one twentieth of the people out of the junior colleges that we should get. What we're going to have to do is subsidize the education of these people.

Even more bleak is the picture painted by Dr. Maurice Mensh, a physician who cares for the Washington, D. C. police:

> This is an uneducated group. You should read some of the essays they write. They can hardly write .... And you put them on the street and ask them to make decisions that are way beyond their capacity.[46]

Moreover, such situations exist even in what are considered to be the most elite, competent and educated police forces in the country. For example, in Berkeley, California, there has recently been a sharp decline in the educational level of recruits.[47]

Alongside problems of recruitment are problems of retention. For example, the *San Francisco Chronicle* reported November 12, 1968, that 195 officers of the San Francisco Police Department had suddenly put in for early retirement. This was approximately 11 percent of the force, which like most urban departments, chronically operates at about 5 percent below authorized strength for lack of suitable applicants. The mass of retirement applications followed the June passage of a ballot proposition to improve policemen retirement benefits and permit retirement at an earlier age. The purpose of the new program was to aid the department in recruiting new officers. Ironically, its results thus far have been to increase retirement applications.

What reason did these policemen give for quitting the force at the earliest possible moment? One veteran inspector said, "It's a dog's job. It's a job the average man wouldn't take. It doesn't have to be, but it is." Another inspector explained his decision this way: "... We're running scared .... If there are social injustices, that's society's bag. We can't cure them. All we can do is make arrests ...." In the judgment of Captain Charles Barca, the men leave because, "It's just an ugly, difficult, uncomfortable way to make a living and will continue to be that way until the general public develops more appreciation for officers and more respect for them."[48]

Although the San Francisco episode was striking because a change in the law produced a sudden mass retirement, reports from urban departments across the nation show that the majority of officers retire as soon as they are eligible.

Even more troubling is the fact that many urban departments report massive resignation rates — often nearly 20 percent per year — among officers short of retirement. According to our interview with Berkeley Police Chief William Beall, Berkeley officers quit the force at all stages of their career. "We lose many veteran officers with ten to fifteen years on the force, men who are at the peak of their efficiency." Almost none of these men take law enforcement jobs elsewhere — Berkeley is one of the highest paying and most admired departments in the nation — but take up other occupations. "The men who find these opportunities are our best, as you would expect," Chief Beall told our interviewer. Thus for many policemen the way to cope with the predicament of modern policing is simply to get out.

One obvious consequence of all this has been a shortage of manpower on police forces. An examination of the Uniform Crime Reports of the Federal Bureau of Investigation shows that the number of full-time police employees per 1,000 population in America's cities has gone virtually unchanged since 1960, while the number of complaints handled by the police has increased enormously.[49] A corollary is, of course, the tendency to overwork and overextend our police.

Training: Deterioration in the Face of New Needs

Perhaps an even more significant effect of pressing manpower needs is the tendency to allow existing training programs to deteriorate because of the pressure for immediate manpower. There is considerable evidence that the new recruits are receiving less adequate training from within departments than in the recent past.[50] However, this deterioration has largely gone unnoticed outside the police. For while police academies have undoubtedly been upgraded in many cities and while their curricula have been immeasurably improved, frequently new recruits are not given the benefit of these improvements. Because of the overwhelming need for manpower, recruits often are hustled out of their training period and onto the streets before they have been adequately instructed. To appreciate the severity of this problem, one need only consider the following excerpts from our interviews with New York policemen about officer training. We select New York because it is the largest police department in the nation and is generally regarded as a police department with outstanding training practices.

A patrolman on a Brooklyn beat:

> There is no professionalization in this department. We're getting a bunch of dummies on this job now. We've got guys out on the street who haven't had any training outside of three or four days in the academy. We had one class that graduated in

December and it had three weeks of training and we had another class that was in June for only I think it was two days, and they were put out on the street. The Mayor says we've got to have more policemen; so we put these guys out, and they shouldn't be there. And they keep saying, we'll send them back to the academy for their training later, and they've said this half a dozen times now and the guys are still out on the street. You know, they aren't even training these guys to shoot.... The way it stands now, we're putting uniforms on guys and calling them cops, but they're not cops; they don't know anything.

A sergeant:

I was an instructor at the police academy last year and I know I had one of my classes turned out on the street after about three weeks. They're supposed to come back to work one day a week at the academy for what they missed, but it never happened. They're out there working now with just three weeks training. Last night I had a couple of young officers who had just a very short time on the job and only a few weeks in the academy and something happened and one of the detectives fired his revolver and one of these young guys couldn't resist, he fired too. I'm really afraid of what's going to happen with these young guys. They're all eager to get in and do what they think is real police work, but they just don't have the training.

A patrolman:

We had a young officer killed about two days ago, and I went and checked on his record myself, so I know this to be a fact. He had been out of the academy for a few months now and he had never had any training on how to handle a gun.

Indeed, according to a story in the *New York Times* more than 2,000 new policemen had been assigned to duty during the first eight months of 1968 without being cleared by the background investigation which "normally precedes appointment to the force."[51] The reason given by city officials was the urgent need to obtain new policemen.

Deterioration of existing training programs is particularly unfortunate at a time when new and vastly improved methods of training are needed if the police are adequately to deal with demonstration, protest and confrontation. In dealing with crowds, police are required to exhibit teamwork, impersonality, and discipline seldom demanded in their routine work. In fact, certain characteristic features of police training may hinder men from operating properly in crowd control situations. As the National Advisory Commission on Civil Disorders observed:

> Traditional police training seeks to develop officers who can work independently and with little direct supervision. But the control of civil disturbances requires quite different performance — large numbers of disciplined personnel, comparable to soldiers in a military unit, organized and trained to work as members of a team under a highly unified command control system. No matter how well-trained and skilled a police officer may be, he will be relatively ineffectual to deal with civil disturbances so long as he functions as an individual.[52]

Thus one National Guard commander complained after viewing the police utilization of Guard units during the Detroit riot of 1967:

> They sliced us up like baloney. The police wanted bodies. They grabbed Guardsmen as soon as they reached the armories, before their units were made up, and sent them out, two on a fire truck, this one on a police car, that one to guard some installation.... The guards simply became lost boys in the big town carrying guns.[53]

Perhaps no more dramatic illustration of the shortcomings of police crowd control techniques can be offered than the Detroit riot of 1967. Responsibility for riot control was divided between U. S. Army paratroopers on one side of town and a combination of Detroit police and the National Guard on the other. The Guard proved as untrained and unreliable as the police and between the two, thousands of rounds of ammunition were expended and perhaps thirty persons were killed while disorder continued. Yet in paratrooper territory, only 201 rounds of ammunition were fired, mostly in the first several hours before stricter fire discipline was imposed, only one person was killed, and within a few hours quiet and order were restored in that section of the city.[54]

The Police View of Protest and Protesters

Faced with the mounting pressures inherent in their job, the police have naturally sought to understand why things are as they are. Explanations which the police, with a few exceptions, have adopted constitute a relatively coherent view of current protests and their causes. The various propositions making up this view have nowhere been set out and made explicit, but they do permeate the police literature. We have tried to set them out as explicitly as possible.

As will be seen, this view functions to justify, indeed, it suggests, a strategy for dealing with protest and protesters. Like any coherent view of events, it helps the police plan what they should do, and understand what they have done. But it must also be said that the police view makes it more difficult to keep the peace and increases the potential for violence. Furthermore, police attitudes toward protest and protesters often lead to conduct at odds with democratic ideals of freedom of speech and political expression. Thus the police often view protest as an intrusion rather than as a contribution to our political processes. In its extreme case, this may result in treating the fundamental political right of dissent as merely an unnecessary inconvenience to traffic, as subversive activity, or both.

The "Rotten Apple" View of Man

What is the foundation of the police view? On the basis of our interviews with police and a systematic study of police publications,[55] we have found that a significant underpinning is what can best be described as a "rotten apple" theory of human nature. Such a theory of human nature is hardly confined to the police, of course. It is widely shared in our society. Many of those to whom the police are responsible hold the "rotten apple" theory, and this complicates the problem in many ways.

Under this doctrine, crime and disorder are attributable mainly to the intentions of evil individuals; human behavior transcends past experience, culture, society, and other external forces and should be understood in terms of wrong choices, deliberately made. Significantly — and contrary to the teachings of all the behavioral sciences — social factors such as poverty, discrimination, inadequate housing, and the like are excluded from the analysis. As one policeman put it simply, "Poverty doesn't cause crime; people do." (And as we discuss later, the policeman's view of "crime" is extremely broad.)

The "rotten apple" view of human nature puts the policeman at odds with the goals and aspirations of many of the groups he is called upon to police. For example, police often relegate social reforms to the category of "coddling criminals," or, in the case of recent ghetto programs, to "selling out" to troublemakers. Moreover, while denying that social factors may contribute to the causes of criminal behavior, police and police publications, somewhat inconsistently, denounce welfare programs not as irrelevant *but as harmful* because they destroy human initiative. This negative view of the goals of policed communities can only make the situation of both police and policed more difficult and explosive. Thus, the black community sees the police not only as representing an alien white society but also as advocating positions fundamentally at odds with its own aspirations. A recent report by the Group for Research on Social Policy at Johns Hopkins University (commissioned by the National Advisory Commission on Civil Disorders) summarizes the police view of the black community:

> The police have wound up face to face with the social consequences of the problems in the ghetto created by the failure of other white institutions — though, as has been observed, they themselves have contributed to those problems in no small degree. The distant and gentlemanly white racism of employers, the discrimination of white parents who object to having their children go to school with Negroes, the disgruntlement of white taxpayers who deride the present welfare system as a sinkhole of public funds but are unwilling to see it replaced by anything more effective — the consequences of these and other forms of white racism have confronted the police with a massive control problem of the kind most evident in the riots.
>
> In our survey, we found that the police were inclined to see the riots as the long-range result of faults in the Negro community — disrespect for law, crime, broken families, etc. — rather than as responses to the stance of the white community. Indeed, nearly one third of the white police saw the riots as the result of what they considered the basic violence and disrespect of

Negroes in general, while only one-fourth attributed the riots to the failure of white institutions. More than three-fourths also regarded the riots as the immediate result of agitators and criminals — a suggestion contradicted by all the evidence accumulated by the riot commission. The police, then, share with the other groups — excepting the black politicians — a tendency to emphasize perceived defects in the black community as an explanation for the difficulties that they encounter in the ghetto.[56]

A similar tension sometimes exists between the police and both higher civic officials and representatives of the media. To the extent that such persons recognize the role of social factors in crime and approve of social reforms, they are viewed by the police as "selling out" and not "supporting the police."

Several less central theories often accompany the "rotten apple" view. These theories, too, are widely shared in our society. First, the police widely blame the current rise in crime on a turn away from traditional religiousness, and they fear an impending moral breakdown.[57] Yet the best recent evidence shows that people's religious beliefs and attendance neither reduce nor increase their propensity toward crime.[58]

But perhaps the main target of current police thinking is permissive childrearing, which many policemen interviewed by our task force view as having led to a generation "that thinks it can get what it yells for." Indeed, one officer interviewed justified the use of physical force on offenders as a corrective for lack of childhood discipline. "If their folks had beat 'em when they were kids, they'd be straight now. As it is, we have to shape 'em up." While much recent evidence, discussed elsewhere in this report, has shown that students most concerned with social issues and most active in protest movements have been reared in homes more "permissive," according to police standards, than those who are uninvolved in these matters, it does not follow that such "permissiveness" leads to criminality. In fact the evidence strongly suggests that persons who receive heavy corporal punishment as children are more likely to act aggressively in ensuing years.[59]

The police also tend to view perfectly legal social deviance, such as long hair worn by men, not only with extreme distaste, but as a ladder to potential criminality. At a luncheon meeting of the International Conference of Police Associations, for example, Los Angeles patrolman George Suber said:

> You know, the way it is today, women will be women — and so will men! I got in trouble with one of them. I stopped him on a freeway after a chase — 95, 100 miles an hour .... He had that hair down to the shoulders.
>
> I said to him, "I have a son about your age, and if you were my son, I'd do two things." "Oh," he said, "what?" "I'd knock him on his ass, and I'd tell him to get a haircut."
>
> "Oh, you don't like my hair?" "No," I said, "you look like a fruit." At that he got very angry. I had to fight him to get him under control.[60]

Noncomformity comes to be viewed with nearly as much suspicion as actual law violation; correspondingly, the police value the familiar, the ordinary, the *status quo* rather than social change. These views both put the police at odds with the dissident communities with whom they have frequent contact and detract from their capacity to appreciate the reasons for dissent, change, or any form of innovative social behavior.

Explaining Mass Protest

It is difficult to find police literature which recognizes that the imperfection of social institutions provides some basis for the discontent of large segments of American society. In addition, organized protest tends to be viewed as the conspiratorial product of authoritarian agitators — usually "Communists" — who mislead otherwise contented people. From a systematic sampling of police literature and statements by law enforcement authorities — ranging from the Director of the Federal Bureau of Investigation to the patrolman on the beat — a common theme emerges in police analyses of mass protest: the search for such "leaders." Again, this is a view, and a search, that is widespread in our society.

Such an approach has serious consequences. The police are led to view protest as illegitimate misbehavior, rather than as legitimate dissent against policies and practices that might be wrong. The police are bound to be hostile to illegitimate misbehavior, and the reduction of protest tends to be seen as their principal goal. Such an attitude leads to more rather than less violence; and a cycle of greater and greater hostility continues.

The "agitational" theory of protest leads to certain characteristic consequences. The police are prone to underestimate both the protesters' numbers and depth of feeling. Again, this increases the likelihood of violence. Yet it is not only the police who believe in the "agitational" theory. Many authorities do when challenged. For example, the Cox Commission found that one reason for the amount of violence when police cleared the buildings at Columbia was the inaccurate estimate of the number of demonstrators in the buildings:

> It seems to us, however, that the Administration's low estimate largely resulted from its inability to see that the seizure of the building was not simply the work of a few radicals but, by the end of the week, involved a significant portion of the student body who had become disenchanted with the operation of the university.[61]

In line with the "agitational" theory of protest, particular significance is attached by police intelligence estimates to the detection of leftists or outsiders of various sorts, as well as to indications of organization and prior planning and preparation. Moreover, similarities in tactics and expressed grievances in a number of scattered places and situations are seen as indicative of common leadership.

Thus Mr. J. Edgar Hoover, in testimony before this commission on September 18, 1968, stated that:

> Communists are in the forefront of civil rights, anti-war, and student demonstrations, many of which ultimately become disorderly and erupt into violence. As an example, Bettina Aptheker Kutzwell, twenty-four year old member of the Communist National Committee, was a leading organizer of the "Free Speech" demonstrations on the campus of the University of California at Berkeley in the fall of 1964.
>
> These protests, culminating in the arrest of more than 800 demonstrators during a massive sit-in, on December 3, 1964, were the forerunner of the current campus upheaval.
>
> In a press conference on July 4, 1968, the opening day of the Communist Party's Special National Convention, Gus Hall,

the Party's General Secretary, stated that there were communists on most of the major college campuses in the country and that they had been involved in the student protests.[62]

Mr. Hoover's statement is significant not only because he was our nation's highest and most renowned law enforcement official, but also because his views are reflected and disseminated throughout the nation — by publicity in the news media and by FBI seminars, briefings, and training for local policemen.

Not surprisingly, then, views similar to Mr. Hoover's dominate the most influential police literature. For instance, a lengthy article in the April, 1965 issue of *The Police Chief*, the official publication of the International Association of Chiefs of Police, concludes, referring to the Berkeley "Free Speech Movement":

> One of the more alarming aspects of these student demonstrations is the ever-present evidence that the guiding hand of communists and extreme leftists was involved.[63]

By contrast, a "blue-ribbon" investigating committee appointed by the Regents of the University of California concluded that:

> We found no evidence that the FSM was organized by the Communist Party, the Progressive Labor Movement, or any other outside group. Despite a number of suggestive coincidences, the evidence which we accumulated left us with no doubt that the Free Speech Movement was a response to the September 14th change in rules regarding political activity at Bancroft and Telegraph, not a pre-planned effort to embarrass or destroy the University on whatever pretext arose.[64]

And more recently, the prestigious Cox Commission, which was headed by the former Solicitor General of the United States and investigated last spring's Columbia disturbances, reported:

> We reject the view that ascribes the April and May disturbances primarily to a conspiracy of student revolutionaries. That demonology is no less false than the naive radical doctrine that attributes all wars, racial injustices, and poverty to the machinations of a capitalist and militarist "Establishment."[65]

One reason why police analysis so often finds "leftists" is that its criteria for characterizing persons as "leftists" is so broad as to be misleading. In practice, the police may not distinguish "dissent" from "subversion." For example, listed in *The Police Chief* article as a "Communist-linked" person is a "former U. S. government employee who, while so employed, participated in picketing the House Committee on Un-American Activities in 1960."[66] Guilt by association is a central analytical tool, and information is culled from such ultra-right publications as *Tocsin* and *Washington Report*. Hostility and suspicion towards the civil rights movement also serves as a major impetus for seeing Communist involvement and leadership. *The Police Chief* found it significant that black civil rights leaders such as James Farmer, Bayard Rustin, John Lewis, James Baldwin and William McAdoo were among "the swarm of sympathizers" who sent messages of support to the FSM.[67]

Some indication of how wide the "communist" net stretches is given by a December, 1968, story in the *Chicago Tribune*. The reporter asked police to comment on the Report of this Commission's Chicago Study Team:

> While most district commanders spoke freely, many policemen declined to comment unless their names were withheld. The majority of these said the Walker report appeared to have been written by members of the United States Supreme Court or Communists.[68]

Supplementing the problem of police definition and identification of leftists is a special vision of the role which such persons play. Just as the presence of police and newsmen at the scene of a protest does not mean they are leaders, so the presence of a handful of radicals should not necessarily lead one to conclude that they are leading the protest movement. Moreover, our chapter on student protest as well as other studies of student protest — including the Byrne Report on the Free Speech Movement and the Cox Report on the Columbia disturbances — indicate that the "leadership," leaving aside for the moment whether it is radical leadership, is able to lead only when events such as administration responses unite significant numbers of students or faculty. For example, the FSM extended over a number of months, and the leaders conducted a long conflict with the university administration and proposed many mass meetings and protests, but their appeals to "sit-in" were heeded by students only intermittently. Sometimes the students rallied by the thousands; at other times the leadership found its base shrunken to no more than several hundred. At these nadir points the leaders were unable to accomplish anything significant; on their own they were powerless. Renewal of mass support for the FSM after each of these pauses was not the work of the leadership, but only occurred when the school administration took actions which aroused mass student feelings of betrayal or inequity. The "leadership" remained relatively constant in its calls for support — and even then had serious internal disputes — but the students gave, withdrew and renewed their support independently, based on events. Clearly, the leaders did not foment student protest on their own; and whatever the intentions or political designs of many FSM leaders, they never had the power to manufacture the protest movement.

One special reason for this kind of police analysis of student protest may derive from police unfamiliarity with the student culture in which such protests occur. When this culture is taken into account, one need not fall back upon theories of sinister outside organizers to explain the ability of students to organize, plan, and produce sophisticated leaders and techniques. Even at the time of the Free Speech Movement in 1964, many of the students, including campus leaders, had spent at least one summer in the South taking part in the civil rights struggles. Moreover, everyone had read about or seen on television, the "sit-ins" and other nonviolent tactics of the civil rights movement. Also, while the police in Berkeley saw the use of loudspeakers and walkie-talkies as evidence of outside leadership, the former had long been standard equipment at student rallies and meetings, and the latter were available in nearby children's toy stores (and were largely a "put on" anyway).Finally, with the intellectual and human resources of thousands of undergraduates, graduate students and faculty at one of the most honored universities in the world, one would hardly expect less competent organization and planning.

A similar analysis may be made of conspiracy arguments relying on similarities in issues and tactics in student protests throughout the nation; explanations more simple than an external organizing force can be found. There is no question that there has been considerable contact among student protesters from many campuses. For example, students who are undergraduates at one university often do graduate work at another. And television news coverage of protest, student newspapers, and books popular in the student culture have long articulated the grievances and tactics around which much unrest revolves. Thus, when it is also considered that students throughout the country do face similar circumstances, it is hardly surprising for similar events to occur widely and to follow a recognizable pattern. Interestingly, collective actions, such as panty raids, have spread through the student subculture in the past without producing sinister conspiracy theories.

A related problem for police is sorting among certain types of claims from and statements about radical movements. Chicago prior to and during the Democratic National Convention is a case in point. To quote from the report of the Commission's Chicago Study Team:

> The threats to the City were varied. Provocative and inflammatory statements, made in connection with activities planned for convention week, were published and widely disseminated. There were also intelligence reports from informants.
>
> Some of this information was *absurd*, like the reported plan to contaminate the city's water supply with LSD. But some were *serious*; and both were strengthened by the authorities *lack of any mechanism for distinguishing one from the other.*
>
> The second factor — the city's *response* — *matched in numbers and logistics at least, the demonstrators' threats.*[69]

Surely it is unsatisfactory not to distinguish the absurd from the serious.[70] And just as surely, the incapacity to distinguish can only result in inadequate protection against real dangers, as well as an increased likelihood of unnecessary suppression and violence. Again, this illustrates some of the problems of the police view when confronted with modern mass protest. The police are more likely to believe that "anarchist" leaders are going to contaminate a city's water supply with LSD than they are to believe that a student anti-war or black protest is an expression of genuine, widespread dissatisfaction. Moreover, some radicals have increasingly learned to utilize and exploit the power of the media in order to stage events and create scenes, to provoke police into attacking peaceful protesters, and the police have played an important role in assuring their success.

An interesting footnote to this discussion of police ideas about protest may be added by noting that, if the standards used by leading police spokesmen to identify a conspiracy were applied to the police themselves, one would conclude that police in the United States constitute an ultra-right wing conspiracy. For example, one would note the growing police militancy with its similar rhetoric and tactics throughout the nation, and the presence of such outside "agitators" as John Harrington, president of the Fraternal Order of Police, at the scene of particular outbursts of militancy. We hasten to add that we do not feel that this is an adequate analysis of the situation. Police, like students, share a common culture and are subject to similar pressures, problems and inequities; the police across the country respond similarly to similar situations because they share common interests, not because they are a "fascist"-led conspiracy.

MILITANCY AS A RESPONSE TO THE POLICE PREDICAMENT: THE POLITICIZATION OF THE POLICE

Introduction

Traditional Political Involvement of Police

Political involvement of the police is not *per se* a new phenomenon. Indeed, it is well known that in the days of the big city political machines the police were in politics in a small way. They often owed their jobs and promotions to the local alderman and were expected to cooperate with political ward bosses and other sachems of the machines. In Albany, writes James Q. Wilson, "The ... Democratic machine dominates the police department as it dominates everything else in the city."[71] In some cities under such domination, police were expected or allowed to cooperate with gamblers or other sources of graft. Wilson comments, however, that "there is little evidence that this is the case in Albany."[72] Still, they played relatively minor roles in active politics. As Wilson writes, "The police are in all cases keenly sensitive to their political environment without in all cases being governed by it."[73] Their political concerns are ordinarily reserved for those decisions affecting their careers as individual members of a bureaucracy.

Yet there was traditionally another — perhaps more significant — way in which the police were political; as the active arm of the status quo. For decades the police were the main bulwark against the labor movement: picket lines were roughly dispersed, meetings were broken up, organizers and activists were shot, beaten, jailed, or run out of town. Such anti-union tactics are unusual today when national labor leaders are firm figures of the establishment, but most of these same men experienced encounters with the police in their youth. While these days have passed for the unions — except perhaps for those having a large Negro membership — participants in the new protest movements of the sixties also have come to see the police as enforcers of the status quo. Civil rights workers, first in the South and then in the North, and subsequently student and anti-war protesters, have met with active police opposition, hostility and force. In addition, as we have discussed elsewhere, minority communities, especially black and Spanish-speaking, have come to regard the police as a hostile army of occupation enforcing the status quo.

While these types of political involvement pose serious questions, recent events point to a new and far more significant politicization of the police. This politicization exacerbates the problems inherent in, for example, using the police to enforce the status quo against minority groups; but, more significantly, it raises questions that are at the very basis of our conception of the role of the police in our society.

The Role of the Police

The importance of police to our legal processes can hardly be overestimated. The police are the interpreters of the legal order to the population; indeed, for many people, they are the sole source of contact with the legal system. Moreover, police are allowed to administer force — even deadly force. Finally, the police make "low visibility" decisions; the nature of the job often allows for the exercise of discretion which is not subject to review by higher authorities. Styles of enforcement vary from place to place, and informality often prevails.[74] So what the policeman does is often perceived as what the law is, and this is not an inaccurate perception.[75]

At the same time, and because he is a law enforcement officer, the policeman is expected to exhibit neutrality in the enforcement of the criminal law, to abide by standards of due process, and to be responsible to higher officials. The concept of police professionalization connotes the further discipline that a profession imposes; and while the police have not yet achieved all of these standards, it is useful to list some of them. For example, one expects a professional group to have a body of specialized knowledge and high levels of education, training, skills, and performance. The peer group should enforce these standards, and elements of state control may even be interjected (as is true, for instance, of doctors and attorneys).

Complicating matters, however, is the policeman's perception of his job, for this may conflict with these demands and expectations. For example, the policeman views himself as an expert in apprehending persons guilty of crimes. Since guilty persons should be punished, he often resents (and may not comply with) rules of procedural due process, seeing them as an administrative obstacle. So also when a policeman arrests a suspect, he most likely has made a determination that the suspect is guilty. Thus it may appear irrational to him to be required to place this suspect in an adjudicatory system which presumes innocence.[76] Moreover, there is a tendency to move from this position to equating "the law" with "the police." One commentator has noted the following:

> In practice, then, the police regard excessive force as a special, but not uncommon, weapon in the battle against crime. They employ it to punish suspects who are seemingly guilty yet unlikely to be convicted, and to secure respect in communities where patrolmen are resented, if not openly detested. And they justify it on the grounds that any civilian, especially any Negro, who arouses their suspicion or withholds due respect loses his

claim to the privileges of law-abiding citizens.[77]

Thus the policeman is likely to focus more on order than on legality and to develop a special conception of illegality.[78] These tendencies are accentuated by and contribute to the growing police frustration, militancy and politicization.

Police Militancy and Politicization: An Overview

The insufficient resources available to the police and a view that attributes unrest to "malcontents" who illegitimately "agitate" persons, in combination with the growing stresses inherent in the policeman's job, led to greater and greater police frustration. And this frustration has increased as the police perceive that some high police and governmental officials and the courts do not accept their prescriptions for social action (such as "unleashing" the police), let alone their demands for more adequate compensation and equipment. In response, the police have become more militant in their views and demands and have recently begun to act out this militancy, sometimes by violence but also by threatening illegal strikes, lobbying, and organizing politically.

This militancy and politicization have built upon an organization framework already available: guild, fraternal, and social organizations. These organizations — especially the guilds — originally devoted to increasing police pay and benefits, have grown stronger. The Fraternal Order of Police, for example, now has 130,000 members in thirty-seven states.[79] Moreover, these organizations have begun to challenge and disobey the authority of police commanders, the civic government, and the courts and to enter the political arena as an organized, militant constituency.

Such developments threaten our long tradition of impartial law enforcement and make the study of "police protest" essential to an understanding of police response to mass protest. Moreover, many of the manifestations of this police activism bring the police themselves into conflict with the legal order — they may act in a manner inconsistent with their role in the legal order, or even illegally. Yet much of this activity is justified in the name of law and order.

The issues raised by the growing police militancy and politicization may at times be made especially difficult and complex because tension exists between our idea of free expression and some of the demands which we must place on the police. In what follows, however, we shall argue that the role of police in a democratic society places special limits on police activism and that, although exact limits are hard to define, in several respects police activism has exceeded reasonable bounds.

It is important to note at this point that not all of our expectations with regard to police behavior are, or should be, reflected in statutes, regulations, or court decisions. We may well expect police to act in ways which would be inappropriate — even impossible — to define in terms of legality and illegality. The issues raised are not necessarily "legal issues," except in the sense that they affect the legal system.[80] Moreover, even where legal issues are involved, it cannot be stressed too much that the solution to problems is not going to be found merely in "strict enforcement" of the law: *solutions* to the problems necessarily will lie in more fundamental sorts of action. Similarly, it is important to understand that the courts in fact can be little more than a generator of ideals. The real problem comes in devising means to infuse these ideals within the administrative structure of police organization. To assert that the courts are an effective check upon police misconduct is often to overlook that misconduct in our desire to affirm the adequacy of our judicial procedures.

Activism in Behalf of Material Benefits

Growing activism is seen both in the issues to which the police address themselves and in the means employed to express these views. A traditional area of police activism is the quest for greater material benefits. Police have long organized into guild-like organizations, such as the Fraternal Order of Police, whose aims include increased wages, pensions, and other benefits. However, difficulties arise when police increase the militancy of their demands. The growing phenomenon of "police protest" is itself a form of mass protest which in many ways directly affects the police response to other protesting groups.

An example of such increased militancy is the threat of a police "strike" in New York by John Cassese, President of the Patrolmen's Benevolent Association.[81] This is not solely a "police issue," but instead is related to the issue of the rights of all government employees. One hardly needs to be reminded of the strikes of transit workers, sanitation workers, teachers, and so forth to realize that the right of government employees to strike is still a disputed issue — in fact, if not in law. Regardless of the merits of the arguments on this general question, it is clear that a police strike is among the most difficult to justify, for the police are clearly in that category of government employment where continued service is necessary not only in the public interest but for the public safety.

And even then the policeman is different; we have seen that, as a law enforcement officer, his role is peculiarly important and sensitive. Thus when police demands for higher material benefits are expressed in a manner defiant of the law, such as illegal strikes, unique problems arise. First, the law enforcement apparatus is placed in the incongruous position of one part having to enforce a law against another part. Even if vigorous enforcement does occur, this is hardly a way to improve the morale and efficiency of the system. Second, efforts to encourage the public to respect and obey laws are seriously undermined. To more people than ever, the law is made to seem arbitrary, subject to the policeman's whim, and lacking in moral force.

Less explicit forms of "strikes" raise related problems. One such tactic is known as the "blue flu." In Detroit last year, for example, according to newspaper accounts, an

> aggressive police association steamrollered city hall into acceptance of one of the most generous salary scales in the nation by the classic tradeunion device of "job action" and "blue flu," police vernacular for phony illnesses that keep police off the job as a display of power.[82]

Ray Girardin, then the police commissioner, was quoted as saying, "I was practically helpless. I couldn't force them to work."[83] "Blue flu" has also been reported elsewhere.[84]

Even more significant, perhaps, is the tactic of varying the enforcement of the criminal law as a means of exerting pressure.

In Detroit the police combined a slowdown in ticket writing with their "blue flu" campaign.[85] New York has experienced this tactic also (although over the issue of one-man patrol cars).[86] Overenforcement of the criminal law can also be used as a tactic of police pressure. Long Island police, for example, are reported to have given unprecedented numbers of traffic tickets in unprecedented circumstances — for such things as exceeding the speed limit by one mile per hour.[87] Even when such conduct stays within the letter of the law, it is correctly perceived by citizens as a non-neutral, political abuse of police power. In this sense it is an even more direct assault on norms of due process and illustrates even more graphically that when the police abuse the law we are left without the machinery to "police the police."

Activism in the Realm of Social Policy

A second substantive area of growing militancy involves broader questions of social policy, including which type of conduct should be criminal, societal attitudes toward protest, the procedural rights of defendants, and the sufficiency of resources allocated to the enforcement of the criminal law. On each of these issues the police are likely to consider themselves expert; after all, they deal in this area day after day.

Police Violence

The most extreme instances of police militancy are seen in confrontations between police and other militant groups, whether they be students, anti-war protesters, or black militants. The police bring to these confrontations their own views on the substantive issues involved, on the character of the protesting groups, and on the desirability and legitimacy of dissent — in other words, the view discussed previously. In numerous instances, including the recent Democratic National Convention in Chicago, the nature of the police response, to quote the Commission's Chicago Study Team, has been "unrestrained and indiscriminate police violence."[88] The extent of this violence has previously been described in some detail.

To understand how it happens one must consider that the police view these other militants as subversive groups who inconvenience the public and espouse dangerous positions. Perhaps some flavor of this feeling is given by the following excerpt from the tape of the Chicago Police Department radio log at 1:29 A.M. Tuesday during the Convention:

> *Police Operator:* 1814, get a wagon over at 1436,
>   We've got an injured hippie.
> *Voice:* 1436 North Wells?
> *Operator:* North Wells.

In quick sequence, there are the following remarks from five other police cars:

"That's no emergency."
"Let him take a bus."
"Kick the fucker."
"Knock his teeth out."
"Throw him in a wastepaper basket."[89]

Similarly, columnist Charles McCabe tells of returning to the lower East Side of New York, his childhood home, and meeting a childhood friend who was now a policeman:

> We went to a corner saloon, together with a couple of buddies and we talked — mostly about cops.
>
> It was really terrifying. These guys, all about my age, had been to Manhattan and Fordham and St. John's. They had brought up decent families. But they had become really quite mad in their work. On the subject of hippies and black militants, they were not really human.
>
> Their language was violent. "If I had my way," said one, "I'd like to take a few days off, and go off somewhere in the country where these bastards might be hanging out, and I'd like to hunt a couple of them down with a rifle." The other cops nodded concurrence. I could only listen.[90]

When these attitudes are coupled with a local government which is also hostile to the protesting group and with provocations by that group, unrestrained police violence is not surprising. Indeed, the police may develop the expectation that such conduct, if not expected, will at least go unpunished. Such may well have been true of the Chicago convention, where the Mayor's negative attitude toward police restraint during the April racial disorders was well known[91] and where discipline against offending police officers was thought unlikely.[92]

Another striking instance of police militancy carried into action is found in the growing number of reports of police attacks on blacks — attacks entirely unrelated to any legitimate police work. Police attacks on members of the militant Black Panther Party are a case in point. In Brooklyn it was reported that off-duty police, plus an undetermined number of other men, attacked several Panthers in a court building where a hearing involving the Panthers was taking place.[93] And in Oakland after the Huey P. Newton trial, two policemen were reported to have shot up a Black Panther office.[94] Moreover, in other cities, including Detroit[95] and San Francisco,[96] off-duty police officers have attacked or shot members of the black community. Accounts of such incidents could continue, but the point is clear; these are isolated episodes only in the trivial sense of being especially clear cut and well-publicized atrocities.

The Revolt Against Higher Authority

Attempts by higher officials to avoid occasions for such outbursts of militancy illustrate the severity of that problem and place in perspective another manifestation of police militancy — the revolt against higher authority. A well-documented example of this phenomenon has been provided by the Commission's Cleveland Investigative Task Force.

The Task Force has found that, in the wake of the July twenty-third shoot-out, police opposition to Mayor Carl Stokes and his administration moved toward open revolt. When police were withdrawn from ghetto duty for one night in order to allow black community leaders to quell the rioting and avoid further deaths, police reportedly refused to answer calls, and some sent racist abuse and obscenities against the Mayor over their radios. Officers in the fifth district flatly refused to travel in two-man squads, one white and one black, into the East Side. For several weeks after the riot, posters with the picture of Mayor Stokes, a Negro, under the words "Wanted for Murder" hung in district stations. Spokesmen for the police officers' wives organization have berated the mayor; the local Fraternal Order of Police has demanded the resignation of Safety Director Joseph F. McNanamon; and many have reportedly been privately purchasing high-powered rifles for use in future riots, despite official opposition by police commanders.

Similar revolts against higher police and civic authority over similar issues have occurred elsewhere. For example, in New York on August 12, 1968, Patrolmen's Benevolent Association President John Cassese instructed his membership, about 99 percent of the force, that if a superior told them to ignore a violation of the law, they should take action notwithstanding that order.[97] Thus if a superior ordered that restraint be used in a particular area of disorder (because, for example, shooting of fleeing looters would create a larger disturbance with which his men could not deal), policemen were to ignore the orders. According to Cassese, this action stemmed from police resentment both of directives to "cool it" during disturbances in the wake of Dr. Martin Luther King's assassination and of restraints during demonstrations the following summer. Cassese charged that the police had been "handcuffed" and were ready for a "direct conflict" with City Hall to end such intereference.[98] Police Commissioner Howard R. Leary countered with a directive of his own reasserting the authority of the departmental chain of command and promising disciplinary action against any officer who refused to obey orders.[99] Thus far the dispute has remained largely rhetorical, and no test incident has yet arisen.[100]

Cassese's position may understate the extent of militancy in the New York police force. According to anonymous sources quoted by Sylvan Fox, *New York Times* reporter and former Deputy Commissioner in Charge of Press Relations for the New York Police Department, Cassese took the steps outlined above in an effort to head off a grass-roots, right-wing revolt within his own organization.[101] "He responded just like the black militants to the guys coming up from below," Fox quotes one informant. "This was an attempt by a union leader to get out in front of his membership." This militant challenge was from the Law Enforcement Group (LEG), some of whose members are alleged to have beaten

Black Panthers outside a Brooklyn courtroom.[102] In fact, it would appear that Cassese was not able to appease these new young militants by his actions. The group has become more and more prominent — the first of the militant, young, right-wing policemen's groups to attract nation-wide attention.

Clearly such militancy is outside any set of norms for police behavior; indeed, it is the antithesis of proper police behavior. Moreover, the implications of such conduct for the political and legal system are profound. The immediate problem, of course, is to find to whom one can turn when the police are outside the law. A corollary is that illegal police behavior will encourage a similar lack of restraint in the general population. Moreover, within the police department itself, the effects of the erosion of authority have untold consequences. A graphic illustration of the loss of discipline and authority which can occur within a police force was recounted by this Commission's Chicago Study Team: "A high-ranking Chicago Police commander admits that on occasion [during the convention disorders] the police 'got out of control.' This same commander appears in one of the most vivid scenes of the entire week, trying desperately to keep an individual policeman from beating demonstrators as he screams, 'For Christ's sake, stop it!'"[103]

Activism and Politicization

A form of police militancy which may raise somewhat different problems is what we have called the politicization of the police — the growing tendency of the police to see themselves as an independent, militant minority asserting itself in the political arena. Conduct in this category may be less extreme than the police lawlessness discussed previously in the sense that it may not necessarily be in violation of the law or departmental orders. On the other hand, the issues it raises are, if anything more complex and far-reaching. Moreover, it exacerbates the problems previously discussed.

Before turning to the more controversial forms of police politicization, we shall focus on the organized police opposition to civilian police review boards, for this experience foreshadowed the later politicization of the police.

Police Solidarity and the Civilian Police Review Boards

The police see themselves, by and large, as a distinct and often deprived group in our society:

> To begin with, the police feel profoundly isolated from a public which, in their view, is at best apathetic and at worst hostile, too solicitous of the criminal and too critical of the patrolman. They also believe that they have been thwarted by the community in the battle against crime, that they have been given a job to do but deprived of the power to do it.[104]

One result of this isolation is a magnified sense of group solidarity. Students of the police are unanimous in stressing the high degree of police solidarity. This solidarity is more than a preference for the company of fellow officers, *esprit de corps*, or the bonds of fellowship and mutual responsibility formed among persons who share danger and stress. It often includes the protective stance adopted regarding police misconduct.[105] A criticism of one policeman is seen as a criticism of all policemen, and thus police tend to unite against complaining citizens, the courts, and other government agencies. Students of police feel that this explains both the speedy exoneration of police when citizen complaints are lodged, and the paucity of reports of misconduct by fellow officers. It seems clear, for example, that the officers who took part in the famous Algiers Motel incident did not expect to get into trouble and that the presence of a State Police Captain did not deter them.[106]

Because of this situation many government officials and citizens have demanded that a means of reviewing police conduct be established and that it be external to the police department. The Civilian Police Review Board is one such recommendation. It, however, is anathema to the police, and fights against these boards marked one of the earliest exertions of political power by the police.

Both because it served as an example for police elsewhere and because of its role in the evolution toward militancy of the police involved, the most significant single case is the Civilian Review

Board battle in New York City.[107] There, in 1966, the largest police force in America, led by the Patrolmen's Benevolent Association, successfully appealed to the public to vote a civilian review board out of existence.

On July 7, 1966, Mayor Lindsay fulfilled a campaign promise by appointing a review board made up of three policemen and four civilians. The PBA placed a referendum on the November ballot to abolish the board. From then until the election the PBA conducted one of the most hardfought and bitter political campaigns in New York City's history. According to a number of accounts policemen campaigned hard while on duty: patrol cars and wagons bore anti-review board signs, police passed out literature, and even harassed persons campaigning on the other side. Many have claimed that at the height of the campaign cars with bumper stickers supporting civilian review were flagrantly ticketed, while an anti-review sticker seemed to make autos almost ticket-proof. Billboards, posters, and ads were heavily exploited and the campaign was heavily financed by the PBA and private sources. One poster depicted damaged stores and a rubble-strewn street and read: "This is the aftermath of a riot in a city that *had* a civilian review board." Included in the test was a statement by J. Edgar Hoover that civilian review boards "virtually paralyzed" the police. Another poster showed a young girl fearfully leaving a subway exit onto a dark street: "The Civilian Review Board must be stopped! ....Her life ... your life ... may depend on it." On November 8, 1966, election night, the civilian review board was buried by a landslide of almost two to one.

Similar battles have since been waged in cities throughout the nation.[108] Our review of printed material circulated by police organizations, articles in police magazines, and speeches by prominent police spokesmen indicates a frequent theme which is fairly represented by the following:

> No matter what names are used by the sponsors of the so-called "Police Review Boards" they exude the obnoxious odor of communism. This scheme is a page right out of the Communist handbook which says in part" ... police are the enemies of communism, if we are to succeed we must do anything to weaken their work, to incapacitate them or make them a subject

of ridicule."[109]

At the outset, it was the distrust by minority group members of internal police review procedures which caused the demands for civilian review boards; the militant opposition of the police has only heightened this distrust. Thus, as might be anticipated, a cycle of greater and greater polarization has been set in motion.

An example of this polarization was seen in St. Louis in September, 1968.[110] The five-man civilian police board suspended one policeman for thirty days and another for ten and sent a letter of reprimand to four others for use of excessive force in a highly controversial arrest and detention of two black militant leaders. While the black community and pro-civil rights whites called this merely a "slap on the wrist," it produced an angry rebellion among rank-and-file police. More than 150 police officers attended an initial protest meeting. A second meeting produced a petition signed by more than 700, one third of the total force, demanding the resignation of the police board and saying police no longer had any confidence in the board. Subsequently, the city has rapidly been polarized. Civil rights and student groups, the ACLU and others have come to the support of the board. Meanwhile the police have built a powerful coalition with unions, neighborhood clubs, political associations, the American Legion, civic groups, and various *ad hoc* committees. In the words of *Los Angeles Times* correspondent D. J. R. Bruckner, the polarization of the community "is a frightening situation."

Beyond the Review Board

Perhaps the most significant impact of these struggles, aside from further polarizing an already polarized situation, has been to give the police a sense of their potential political power. Their overwhelming victories in review board fights have given them, as one distinguished law professor interviewed by a Task Force member put it, "a taste of blood." Indeed, many experts believe the American police will never be the same again. Police organizations such as the Patrolmen's Benevolent Association, conceived of originally as combining the function of a trade union and lobbying organization for police benefits, are becoming vehicles for the political sentiments and aspirations of the police rank and file, as well as a rallying point for organized opposition to higher police and civilian authority. We call this phenomenon the politicization of the police.

On issues concerning the criminal law and its enforcement, the police traditionally have asserted their views by communications within the existing police structure and by testimony before legislative and executive policy-making bodies. Today, as a result of their growing politicization, the police are more likely to resort to activist forms of expression such as lobbying and campaign support for measures and candidates conforming to their ideology. Indeed, at a time when they are becoming more and more disenchanted with the decisions reached by our political process, the police perceive no sharp line dividing traditional activities from more partisan political issues such as choices among candidates for local or national office.

One example of partisan political involvement was found in the last two Presidential campaigns. During the 1964 campaign a number of departments had to issue special directives in order to curtail policemen from wearing Goldwater buttons on their uniforms and putting Goldwater stickers on their patrol cars. Moreover, this last fall there were reports that police in Washington, D.C., and other cities were passing out Wallace-for-President literature from police patrol cars.[111]

But perhaps the most significant political action is seen on the local level, and this political activity is far from the traditional seeking of higher benefits. According to Michael Churns, one of the founders of the Law Enforcement Group in New York, his group is more interested in "constitutional and moral" issues than "the purely monetary considerations. We're for better conditions in the country."[112] A survey of police in five cities found that police "are coming to see themselves as the political force by which radicalism, student demonstrations, and Black Power can be blocked.[113]

This activity takes many forms, one of which is campaign support. The following excerpt from a story in the *San Francisco Chronicle* reveals a practice which is becoming more common across the nation:

> Plans were announced yesterday to have policemen from all
> communities in Alameda County sell $10-a-person tickets for a
> testimonial dinner for Robert Hannon, Republican candidate
> for State Senate.
>
> Detective Sergeant Jack Baugh of the Alameda County Sher-
> iff's Department, co-chairman of the dinner, said the record of
> Democratic State Senator Nicholas Petris is "repulsive to a po-
> lice officer."
>
> Baugh said tickets would be sold by police outside of their
> working hours and in civilian clothing.[114]

Police are also discovering that as a lobby they can have great
political power. Mayor John Lindsay has seen this power in New
York. When he tried to have police cadets take over traffic patrol
duties in New York, the Patrolmen's Benevolent Association lobbied against him in the state legislature and won.[115] On other
issues, such as the use of one-man squad cars and the consolida-
tion of precincts, the mayor has had to back down.[116] Indeed, the
PBA may well be one of the most powerful lobbies in the New
York State Legislature. The scale of its activities is indicated by a
reception held in March, 1968 for members of the state legislature.[117] More than 500 people were entertained in the Grand Ball-
room of the DeWitt Clinton Hotel in Albany by three bars, a live
orchestra, and similar trappings. The success of PBA lobbying is
seen, again, in the fact that, after a bitter fight, the New York State
Legislature, at the urging of the PBA, broadened the areas in
which police may use deadly force.

A powerful police lobby is not unique to New York. In Boston,
for example, the PBA lobbied vigorously against Mayor Kevin
White's decision to place civilians in most jobs occupied by traffic
patrolmen, a move which would have freed men for crime work.
The City Council, which had to approve the change, sided with
the police.[118] The mayor then went to the state legislature, but the
police lobby again prevailed and White lost. In November 1968,
the PBA again prevailed over the mayor when the City Council
substantially altered the police component of White's Model
Cities Program. Changes included the removal of a plan to allow
citizens to receive (not judge) complaints against the police and
the deletion of references to the need to recruit blacks to the police

force.[119]

In a West Coast city in which we conducted interviews, a graphic example of police lobbying was described. According to a policeman on the board of the local Police Officers Association, the practice has been to put "pressure on city council members directly through phone calls, luncheons, and the like. So far the local POA leaders are uncertain how far this has gotten them. As one POA board member told a Task Force interviewer: "[We have gotten very little] although we have tried to wine and dine them and even blackmail the members of the city council. But they are too stupid to understand what the Association is trying to do."

Militant tactics similar to those used by students, anti-war protesters, and blacks have also found their way into police activism. For example, New York police have marched on City Hall, and Detroit police have shown up in uniform at a city council hearing in what some councilmen are reported to have felt was a blatant attempt at intimidation.[120] Moreover, because they are law enforcement officers, police can avail themselves of tactics beyond those available to most dissident groups — and of even more questionable legitimacy. The examples of slowdowns in ticket writing and overenforcement of the criminal law have already been discussed. In addition, an extraordinary tactic has been reported in a confrontation between Philadelphia Police Commissioner Frank L. Rizzo and the city's school board over the stationing of police in unruly, predominantly black schools. Rizzo is said to have told the school board that the police performed many duties of which the public was unaware — for example, keeping "dossiers" on a lot of people including "some of you school people."[121] The threat was left implicit. Similarly, a private Los Angeles group called "Fi-Po," the Fire and Police Research Association, maintains dossiers on individuals and groups, compiled from "open sources." During the 1968 campaign Fi-Po is reported to have passed the word that the son of a candidate for a major California political office had once been arrested on a narcotics charge.[122]

One of the more militant police groups in New York is "LEG," the Law Enforcement Group. Its activism is not only political but is often directed against the courts. The hostility of police to the

United States Supreme Court — and their disregard of some of its rulings — is widely known.[123] LEG, however, directs much of its attention to lower courts. Indeed, it came into existence with a petition calling for the removal of Criminal Court Judge John F. Furey from the bench because LEG alleged he permitted unruly conduct in his court during the arraignment of two members of the Black Panther Party.[124]

As pointed out previously, the police tend to view themselves as society's experts in the determination of guilt and the apprehension of guilty persons. Because they also see themselves as an abused and misunderstood minority, they are particularly sensitive to what they perceive as challenges to "their system of criminal justice — whether by unruly Black Panthers or "misguided" judges.

LEG's current political activities are varied. They are demanding a grand jury investigation of "coddling" of criminals in the courts.[125] And moving more explicitly into the realm of partisan politicis, LEG announced a campaign to support United States Senators who will prevent "another Warren Court" by blocking the appointment of Abe Fortas as Chief Justice.[126] But perhaps LEG's most extraordinary tactic is its system of court watchers. Off-duty members attend court sessions and note "misbehavior" by judges, prosecutors, probation officers, and others involved in the judicial process. Lieutenant Leon Laino, one of the founders of LEG, described this program to a Task Force interviewer:

> The courts have a lot to do with the crime rate in the way they handle people, let them out on bail or without bail so that they can commit the same crime two or three times before coming to trial. Nowadays the courts let people get away with anything. Even disrespectful conduct while in court. But since we have instituted a policy of court watchers ... we have noticed a change in the behavior of these judges.

LEG has already signaled out several judges as "coddlers" of criminals.[127] Especially where judges must stand for reelection, the potential for further police intervention into the judicial and electoral process appears clear.

Although the politicization of the police is recent and thus difficult to assess, one thing is clear — police political power in our large cities is both considerable and growing. The police are quite consciously building this power, and its impact is being felt throughout the political system. An example is given by an observer in New York:

> In fact, there's a growing danger of disagreeing with the cops. On precinct consolidation, for example, councilmen, rabbis, state senators privately would say "It doesn't sound like a bad idea, but the police are getting everybody so hot, I don't see how we could go with it."
>
> See, these [issues like precinct consolidation] are not the exciting issues and a lot of people don't feel like taking on a political force like the cops.[128]

Some police spokesmen rate this power even higher:

> We could elect governors, or at least knock 'em off. I've told them [the police] if you get out and organize, you could become one of the strongest political units in the commonwealth.[129]

And in cities, including New York[130] and Boston[131] there is talk that police spokesmen may run for public office.

Thus the growing police politicization, combined with the disruptive potential of other forms of police militancy, make the police a political force to be reckoned with in today's city. Indeed at times they appear to dominate. For example, aides to New York Mayor John Lindsay are reported to feel that the mayor's office has lost the initiative to the police, who now dominate the public dialogue.[132] And some observers feel that ultimate political power in Philadelphia resides in Police Commissioner Frank L. Rizzo, not the mayor.[133] The implications of this situation are pointed to by Boston Mayor Kevin White:

> Are the police governable? Yes. Do I control the police, right now? No.[134]

The Military Analogy

Political involvement of the police — even apart from its contribution to more radical forms of police militancy — raises serious problems. First, aside from the military, the police have a practical monopoly on the legal use of force in our society.

For just such a reason our country has a tradition of wariness toward politicization of its armed forces, and thus both law and custom restrict the political activities of members of the military. Similar considerations obviously apply to the police.

In some senses the police are an even greater source of potential concern than the armed forces because of their closeness to the day-to-day workings of the politicial process and their frequent interaction with the population. These factors make police abuse of the political process a more immediate prospect. For example, bumper stickers on squad cars, political buttons on uniforms, selective ticketing and similar contacts with citizens quickly impart a political message.

A second factor which has led to restrictions on members of the armed forces is the fear that unfettered political expression, if adopted as a principle, might in practice lead to political coercion *within* the military. Control over promotions and disciplinary action could make coercion possible, and pressure might be exerted on lower ranking members to adopt, contribute to, or work for a particular political cause. Thus, again, regulation (and sometimes prohibition) of certain political activities has been undertaken. For example, superiors are prohibited from soliciting funds from inferiors, and many political activities are prohibited while in uniform or on duty. Such considerations again apply to the police.

The Judicial Analogy

Even where coercion of the populace (or fellow force members) does not exist in fact, politicization of the police may create the appearance of such abuses. This can affect the political process and create both hostility toward the police and disrespect for the legal and political system.

Moreover, lobbying, campaigning and the like, in and of themselves, tend to make the policing function itself appear politically motivated and nonneutral. Since the policing function is for so many people so central and important a part of our legal mechanisms, the actual or apparent politicization of policing would carry over to perceptions of the entire legal system. Such perceptions of politicization would be contrary to society's view that the system should be neutral and nonpolitical. And such a situation would, of course, have adverse consequences for confidence in and thus reliance on its legal system to resolve disputes peacefully. And this is most true of those groups — student, anti-war protesters, and blacks — who perceive the police political position as most hostile to their own aspirations and who are also among the most heavily policed. Moreover, the legal system would in turn be exposed to even greater political pressures than is presently the case.

So, while the police may be analogous to other government employees or to members of the armed forces, they are also, and perhaps more importantly, analogous to the judiciary. Each interprets the legal order to and imposes the legal [order] on the population, and thus the actions of each are expected to be neutral and nonpolitical. In the case of the judiciary, there is a strong tradition of removing them from the partisan political arena lest their involvement impede the functioning of the system.

It may be useful in this connection to illustrate just how strong are our societal norms concerning judicial behavior and to note that these norms often demand standards of conduct higher than what is legally required. For example, even when judges run for reelection, it is widely understood that the election should not be political in the usual sense. Moreover, at various times in our history there has been public uneasiness about justices of the Supreme Court advising presidents of the United States. Perhaps even more to the point, however, is the fact that whereas justices have from time to time informally advised presidents, it is unthinkable that they would take to the stump or engage in overt political activity in their behalf.

CONCLUSION

Thus we find that the policeman in America is overworked, undertrained, underpaid, and undereducated. His difficulties are compounded by a view expounded at all law enforcement levels — from the Director of the Federal Bureau of Investigation to the patrolman on the beat. This view gives little consideration to the effects of such social factors as poverty and discrimination and virtually ignores the possibility of legitimate social discontent. Typically, it attributes mass protest instead to a conspiracy promulgated by agitators, often Communists, who misdirect otherwise contented people. This view, disproven so many times by scholars and distinguished commissions, tends to set the police against dissident groups, however lawful.

Given their social role and their view, the police have become increasingly frustrated, alienated, and angry. These feelings are being expressed in a growing militancy and political activism.

In short, the police are protesting. Police slowdowns and other forms of strike activity, usually of questionable legality, are employed to gain greater material benefits or changes in governmental policy (such as the "unleashing of the police"). Moreover, direct police challenges to departmental and civic authority have followed recent urban disorders, and criticisms of the judiciary have escalated to "court watching" by police.

These developments are a part of a large phenomenon — the emergence of the police as a self-conscious, independent political power. In many cities and states the police lobby rivals even duly elected officials in influence. This poses serious problems; for police — just as courts — are expected to be neutral and nonpolitical — even the appearance of partiality impairs public confidence in the legal system. Thus, difficult though it may be to articulate standards for police conduct, the present police militancy seems to have exceeded reasonable bounds.

Moreover, this police militancy is hostile to the aspirations of other dissident groups in our society. Police view students, the anti-war protesters, and blacks as a danger to our political system, and racial prejudice pervades the police attitudes and actions. No government institution appears so deficient in its understanding of the constructive role of dissent in a constitutional democracy as the police.

Thus, it should not be surprising that police response to mass protest has resulted in a steady escalation of conflict, hostility, and violence. The police violence during the Democratic National Convention in Chicago was not a unique phenomenon — we have found numerous instances where violence has been initiated or exacerbated by police actions and attitudes. Such police violence is the antithesis of both law and order. It leads only to increased hostility, polarization, and violence — both in the immediate situation and in the future. Certainly it is clear today that effective policing ultimately depends upon the cooperation and goodwill of the policed, and these resources are quickly being exhausted by present police attitudes and practices.

Implicit in this analysis is a recognition that the problems discussed in this chapter derive from larger defects. Their importance reflects the urgent need for the fundamental reforms discussed elsewhere in this report — reforms leading, for example, to more responsive political institutions and an affirmation of the right to dissent.

Police spokesmen, in assessing their occupation, conclude that what they need is more money and manpower and less interference by the civic government and the courts. As this chapter has indicated, the latter recommendation is mistaken, and the former does not say enough. What is needed is a major transformation of the police culture by, for example, bringing a greater variety of persons into police work and providing better training. Because of time limitations, this Task Force has not developed specific proposals for legislative or executive action. We have, however, given thought to such proposals, and in what follows we shall discuss the types of action we feel should be taken.

A first step is a thorough appraisal by the Department of Justice of the role played by the federal government in the development of the current police view of protest and protesters. This would require several efforts, including examining and evaluating literature distributed by the federal government to local police agencies and examining all programs sponsored by the federal government for the education of police. Moreover, an attempt should be made to create an enlightened curriculum for police training concerning the role of political activity, demonstration, and protest in a constitutional democracy.

A second step toward a meaningful transformation of the police culture would be the establishment of a Social Service Academy under the sponsorship of the United States government. This Academy should be governed by an independent board whose members would be selected for their eminence in such fields as criminology, sociology, and psychology — in a manner analogous to that used for the selection of members of the National Science Board of the National Science Foundation.[135] Like the military academies, this institutuion would provide a free higher education to prospective police, social workers, and urban specialists who, after graduation, would spend a minimum of three or four years in their chosen specialty. Internships would be arranged during one or more summers, and police graduates would undoubtedly be considered qualified to enter police departments at an advanced level. The academy would provide the prospective policeman an opportunity for the equivalent of a college education. Moreover, it would attract a larger variety of people into police work — and help bring a desirable flexibility in dominant police culture. This suggestion might be supplemented within existing universities by a federally financed program of scholarships and loans to persons who commit themselves to a period of police, social welfare or urban work after graduation (or a forgiving of educational loans to persons who in fact enter such occupations). Indeed, this nation has in the past adopted analogous programs[136] when the need in question was national defense.

Accompanying the creation of a Social Service Academy should be the development of a system of lateral entry in police departments. This has been recommended numerous times in the past,[137] and we can only urge that consideration be given to a program of federal incentives to achieve this end. Generally speaking, across the country one police department cannot hire a man from another police department unless that man starts at the bottom.[138] The only exception is in the hiring of police chiefs. This situation is analogous to a corporation which filled its executive positions exclusively with persons who had begun their careers with that corporation. One can imagine how dismal the corporate scene would be if inbreeding were the fundamental and unshakable norm in the acquisition of personnel. This is the situation in most police departments.

The combination of these two programs would no doubt lead to increased pay for police. Lateral entry itself would tend, through the market mechanism, to drive wages up, and the insertion of academy-trained recruits into the labor pool would have the same result. The quality of people and training which we envision should go a long way toward making policing a profession, in the full sense of that term. As this result is approached, substantial increases in police pay would be necessary and desirable, and these increases should be significantly more than the 10 or 15 percent usually mentioned.

The impact of these changes will be felt only over a period of perhaps ten years. Yet a short-run means to alleviate the problems discussed above is a necessity. Several possibilities exist. First, the lack of police manpower is in part due to a problem of definition. Certain functions which the police now perform, such as traffic control, could be performed by other civil servants. Other writers and commissions have recommended such a redefinition of the "police function," and we concur.

In need of similar re-examination is the definition of "crime." This is not the best of all possible worlds, and resources are limited. Thus even disregarding the philosophical debate over legislation in the area of "private morality," a rational allocation of police resources might well remove certain conduct from the purview of the criminal law.[139] Not only would such action free police resources for more important uses, but it would also remove one source of police corruption and public disrespect for law.

If communities are to be policed adequately — and this concept includes the community's acceptance of the policing as well as the quality of the policing — the principle of community control of the police seems inescapable. Local control of the police is a fairly well-established institution in the suburbs, and it may well be a necessity in the central cities. We recognize that the implementation of this policy is a complex matter — that different plans would be appropriate in different urban situations and that different types of control for different police functions may be desirable. We feel, however, that the principle is sound and that alternative models should be developed and utilized.

Finally, institutionalized grievance procedures are badly needed, especially in our large cities. It is clear that effective machinery should be external to any offending governmental agency if it is to be effective *and* perceived as effective.[140] Ideally, the police should not be singled out for such treatment, but it is imperative that they be included. We suggest that models for a federal grievance procedure be explored.

NOTES

1. James Baldwin, *Nobody Knows My Name* (New York: Dell, 1962), pp. 65-67.
2. *Report of the National Advisory Commission on Civil Disorders* (New York: Bantam Books, 1968). See especially "The Background of Disorder," pp. 135-150 and the charts on pp. 149-150.
3. See, e.g., Robert M. Fogelson, "From Resentment to Confrontation: The Police, the Negroes, and the Outbreak of the Nineteen-Sixties Riots," *Political Science Quarterly*, LXXXIII, No. 2 (June 1968), pp. 217-247.
4. Among these are: William A. Westley, *The Police: A Sociological Study of Law, Custom and Morality* (unpublished Ph.D. dissertation, Department of Sociology, University of Chicago, 1951); Jerome H. Skolnick, *Justice Without Trial* (New York: Wiley, 1966); Arthur Niederhoffer, *Behind the Shield: The Police in Urban Society* (New York: Doubleday, 1967); Burton Levy, "Cops in the Ghetto: A Problem of the Police System," *American Behavioral Scientist* (March-April, 1968), pp. 31-34.
5. Miami Study Team on Civil Disturbances, *Miami Report*, submitted to this Commission, January 15, 1969.
6. Unpublished report prepared by the Mayor's Commission on Conditions in Harlem (New York, 1935), *The Negro in Harlem*.
7. Westley, p. 168.
8. "Patterns of Behavior in Police and Citizen Transactions."
9. This and subsequent interview information were derived from interviews carried out by members of this task force, unless otherwise indicated.
10. Robert Conot, *Rivers of Blood, Years of Darkness* (New York: Bantam, 1967).
11. "Book 5" (Washington: U. S. Government Printing Office, 1961), p. 28.
12. See, e. g., Ed Cray, *The Big Blue Line: Police Power vs. Human Rights* (New York: Coward-McCann, 1967); J. H. Skolnick, "The Police and the Urban Ghetto," *Research Contributions of the American Bar Foundation*, 1968, no. 3 (Chicago: American Bar Foundation, 1968); Anthony Amsterdam, Testimony to the National Commission on Causes and Prevention of Violence, *Transcript of Proceedings*, especially pp. 2476, 2485, 2491; Paul Chevigny, *Police Power* (New York: Pantheon, 1969); Report of the National Advisory Commission on Civil Disorders; "Task Force Report: The Police," *The President's Commission on Law*

Enforcement and Administration of Justice (Washington: U. S. Government Printing Office, 1967), pp. 148, 164, 181-183.

13. According to the *San Francisco Chronicle* on November 5, 1968, p. 4, and the *Detroit Free Press*, November 14, 1968, nine police were suspended for beating black youths at a dance.

14. An off-duty policeman was indicted for shooting a black truck driver following a minor traffic accident, *San Francisco Sunday Chronicle and Examiner, This World*, October 13, 1968, pp. 5-6. He was later acquitted.

15. As reported in the *New York Times*, September 5, 1968, p. 1, 150 off-duty policemen attacked a group of Negroes — some members of the Black Panthers — in a hallway of the Brooklyn Criminal Courts Building.

16. On-duty policemen were dismissed after firing over twelve shots into a Black Panther headquarters, *San Francisco Chronicle*, September 11, 1968, p. 1.

17. In Newark National Guardsmen and state troppers "were directing mass fire at the Hayes Housing Project in response to what they believed were snipers" (Report of the National Advisory Commission, pp. 67-67) although the only shots fired were by Guardsmen. The same pages describe the shooting up of stores with the sign "Soul Brother" in their windows. In Detroit, "Without any clear authorization or direction someone opened fire upon the suspected building. A tank rolled up and sprayed the building with .50 caliber tracer bullets." (Report of the National Advisory Commission, p. 97).

18. In Paternson, New Jersey, according to the *New York Times*, October 30, 1968, p. 18, a grand jury placed blame on Paterson police for vandalism, brutality, and intimidation in quelling a week of racial disorder. Amsterdam refers to such police tactics as "terrorization as a means of crowd control" in his testimony, p. 2491.

19. Fact-finding Commission Appointed to Investigate the Disturbances at Columbia University in April and May, 1968, The Cox Commission, *Crisis at Columbia* (New York: Vintage, 1968). See also Chapter III of this report and Daniel Bell, "Columbia and the New Left," *The Public Interest* (Fall 1968).

20. April 27 Investigating Committee, Dr. Edward J. Sparling, Chairman, *Dissent and Disorder: A Report of the Citizens of Chicago on the April 27 Peace Parade*, August 1, 1968.

21. *Rights in Conflict* (Chicago, November 18, 1968), p. vii; this report is now available in trade editions; for example, New York: Bantam Books, 1968.

22. *Ibid.*

23. *New York Times*, March 23-25, 2968.

24. *New York Times*, April 28, 29, 1968.

25. Los Angeles: Sawyer Press, 1967.

26. Ibid., "Introduction."

27. *Dissent and Disorder*, pp. 30-31.

28. Mayor Richard J. Daley, "Strategy of Confrontation," published as a

Special Section in the *Chicago Daily News*, September 9, 1968.

29. October 28, 1968, p. 3.

30. "A Policeman Looks at Crime," U. S. News and World Report, August 1, 1966, p. 52.

31. November 16, 1968, p. 28.

32. *Ibid.*

33. See, e.g., Michael Banton, *The Policeman in the Community* (London: Tavistock Publications, 1964), p. 7 and Arthur L. Stinchcombe, "Institutions of Privacy in the Determination of Police Administrative Practices," *American Journal of Sociology*, LXIX (September, 1963), pp. 150-160, both cited and discussed in Skolnick, *Justice Without Trial*, p. 33.

34. James Q. Wilson, *Varieties of Police Behavior* (Cambridge, Mass: Harvard University Press, 1968), p. 49. The original is in italics.

35. *Behind the Shield*, pp. 103-52.

36. John H. McNamara, "Uncertainties in Police Work: The Relevance of Police Recruits' Backgrounds and Training," in *The Police: Six Sociological Essays*, ed. David J. Bordua (New York: John Wiley, 1967), pp. 163-252.

37. According to Richard Wade, a University of Chicago professor of urban history, "Fifty years ago, policemen had an income relatively higher than other trades and there were more applicants than there were jobs;" quoted in A. James Reichley, "The Way to Cool the Police Rebellion," *Fortune* (December, 1968), p. 113.

38. Interviews in San Francisco have shown that a new recruit faces twelve years of night work before he is "promoted" to daylight work. This undoubtedly is one explanation.

39. *Behind the Shield* ..., p. 16.

40. Evidence indicates that concurrent with the relative decline in financial rewards for police, the quantity and quality of equipment in some departments has also declined.

41. *Behind the Shield* ... , p. 16.

42. Reichley, p. 113.

43. Police salaries average only two-thirds that of union plumbers, *Time*, October 4, 1968, p. 27.

44. *Time*, October 4, 1968, pp. 26-27; Sandy Smith, "The Mob: You Can't Expect Police on the Take to Take Orders," *Life*, December 6, 1968, pp. 40-43.

45. Today, according to Reichley, fewer than ten percent of the policemen are college graduates when recruited to the force; most have not more than a high school diploma. And *Time* reported that Detroit recruits are from the bottom twenty-five percent of high school graduating classes, October 4, 1968, p. 26.

46. *Washington Post*, December 15, 1968, p. B3.

47. Interview with Police Chief William Beall.

48. Quotes from *San Francisco Examiner*, November 13, 1968, pp. 1, 16.

49. In 1960 there were 1.9 police employees per 1,000 population; in 1966, this ratio had increased to 2.0 employees per thousand. At the same time the number of serious criminal offenses increased 48.4% in just the six-year period from 1960-66. Thus, while the number of indexed crimes jumped almost 50%, the number of employees was augmented by no more than 5%. J. Edgar Hoover, Director, Federal Bureau of Investigation, *Uniform Crime Reports for the United States, 1960, 1966* (Washington: U. S. Department of Justice, U. S. Government Printing Office).

50. Charles Saunders, Jr. of the Brookings Institution reports that some departments won't allow new officers to issue tickets — presumably because they have not undergone sufficient training — but require them to carry guns, Reichley, p. 150.

51. August 30, 1968, p. 10.

52. Report of the National Advisory Commission, p. 485.

53. G. Wills, *The Second Civil War* (New York: New American Library, 1968), p. 47.

54. See Report of the National Advisory Commission, p. 100.

55. Among numerous other publications *Law and Order* and *The Police Chief* magazines for the past eighteen months were reviewed. We read them both for an understanding of the police perspective of their world and for their theories of appropriate response to social problems. Interviews and other reports augmented this study.

56. David Boesel, Richard Berk, W. Eugene Groves, Bettye Eidson, Peter H. Rossi, "White Institutions and Black Rage," *Trans*-action (March 1969), p. 31.

57. See, e.g., J. Edgar Hoover, quoted in John Edward Coogan, "Religion a Preventive of Delinquency," *Federal Probation*, XVIII (December 1954), p. 29.

58. Travis Hirschi and Rodney Stark, "Hellfire and Delinquency," publication A-96, Survey Research Center, University of California at Berkeley.

59. See, e.g., R. R. Sears, et. al., "Some Child-rearing Antecedents of Aggression and Dependency in Young Children," *Genetic Psychology Monograph* (1953), pp. 135-234; E. Hollenberg and M. Sperry, "Some Antecedents of Aggression and Effects of Frustration in Doll Play," *Personality* (1951), pp. 32-43; W. C. Becker, et al., "Relations of Factors Derived from Parent Interview Ratings to Behavior Problems of Five Year Olds," *Child Development*, XXXIII (1962), pp. 509-35; and M. L. Hoffman, "Power Assertion by the Parent and Its Impact on the Child," *Child Development*, XXXI (1960), pp. 129-43.

60. *Washington Post*, December 15, 1968, p. B3.

61. Cox Commission, p. 164.

62. *Proceedings*, p. 56.

63. The Police Chief, April, 1965, p. 10.

64. The Byrne Commission report submitted to the Special Committee of The Regents of the University of California on May 7, 1965; most easily available in *Los Angeles Times*, May 12, 1965, Part IV, pp. 1-6. Quoted section, p. 5.

65. Cox Commission, p. 189.

66. *The Police Chief*, April, 1965, p. 36.

67. *Ibid.*, pp. 42-44.

68. Donald Yabush, *Chicago Tribune*, December 3, 1968, p. 1.

69. Chicago Study Team, pp. vii-viii, emphasis added.

70. This variety of intelligence received by law enforcement officials is indicated by this listing of Yippie threats published in the mass media: "There were reports of proposals to dynamite natural gas lines; to dump hallucinating drugs into the city's water system; to print forged credentials so that demonstrators could slip into the convention hall; to stage a mass stall-in of old jalopies on the expressways and thereby disrupt traffic; to take over gas stations, flood sewers with gasoline, then burn the city; to fornicate in the parks and on Lake Michigan's beaches; to release greased pigs throughout Chicago, at the Federal Building and at the Amphitheatre; to slash tires along the city's freeways and tie up traffic in all directions; to scatter razor sharp three-inch nails along the city's highways; to place underground agents in hotels, restaurants, and kitchens where food was prepared for delegates, and drug food and drink; to paint cars like independent taxicabs and forceably take delegates to Wisconsin or some other place far from the convention; to engage Yippie girls as "hookers" to attract delegates and dose their drinks with LSD; to bombard the Amphitheatre with mortars from several miles away; to jam communication lines from mobile units; to disrupt the operations of airport control towers, hotel elevators and railway switching yards; to gather 230 'hyperpotent' hippie males into a special battalion to seduce the wives, daughters and girlfriends of convention delegates; to assemble 100,000 people to burn draft cards with the fires spelling out: 'Beat Army;' to turn on fire hydrants, set off false fire and police alarms, and string wire between trees in Grant Park and Lincoln Park to trip up three-wheeled vehicles of the Chicago police; to dress Yippies like Viet Cong and walk the streets shaking hands or passing out rice; to infiltrate the right wing with short haired Yippies and at the right moment exclaim: 'You know, these Yippies have something to say!;" to have ten thousand nude bodies floating on Lake Michigan — the list could go on." Chicago Study Team, p. 49.

71. Wilson, *Varieties of Police Behavior*, pp. 237-238.

72. P. 238.

73. P. 230.

74. See Wilson generally.

75. See, e.g., Wayne R. LaFave, *Arrest: The Decision to Take a Suspect into Custody* (Chicago: American Bar Foundation, 1965); Skolnick, *Justice*

Without Trial, and Wilson, *Varieties of Police Behavior.*

76. A cornerstone of our judicial system is that an accused is presumed innocent until proven guilty. The policeman, however, may feel that this should not be the rule since he would not have arrested the accused unless he was guilty. For a more detailed discussion of these points, see Skolnick, *Justice Without Trial,* Chapter 9, pp. 182-203.

77. Fogelson, p. 226.

78. We have discussed previously the tendency to equate defiance with crime.

79. Interview with John Harrington, President of the Fraternal Order of Police.

80. Certain political activities by police — discussed in detail below — may raise such issues, especially where the activities create sharp antagonism within the policed community and threaten the ability of the civic government to control the police.

81. A "job action" began in response to the City's refusal "to negotiate a new contract." (*New York Times,* October 16, 1968, p. 1). On October 26, the *New York Times* reported that Cassese was in defiance of a court order in his direction to continue the "slowdown," (p. 1). But on October 27, it was reported that he had bowed to the court order (*New York Times,* p. 1).

82. *San Francisco Chronicle,* December 16, 1968, p. 12.

83. *Washington Post,* December 15, 1968, p. B1.

84. For example, in Newark, New Jersey, as reported in *New York Times,* November 30, 1968, p. 1.

85. *Washington Post,* Demceber 15, 1968, p. B1.

86. *Ibid.*

87. *New York Times,* November 18, 1968, p. 1.

88. Chicago Study Team, p. vii.

89. Chicago Study Team, p. 117.

90. *San Francisco Chronicle,* December 11, 1968, p. 41.

91. Chicago Study Team, p. 1.

92. The Chicago Study Team writes that almost three months after the convention no disciplinary action had been taken against most of the police violators, (p. xiii).

93. *New York Times,* September 5, 1968, p. 1.

94. *San Francisco Chronicle,* September 11, 1968, p. 1.

95. *San Francisco Chronicle,* November 5, 1968, p. 4, and *Detroit Free Press,* November 14, 1968.

96. *San Francisco Sunday Chronicle and Examiner,* This World, October 13, 1968, pp. 5-6.

97. *Los Angeles Times,* August 16, 1968, p. 4.

98. *New York Times,* August 18, 1968, p. E7.

99. *Los Angeles Times,* August 16, 1968, p. 4.

100. According to a *Washington Post* story, the PBA may have backed down. December 15, 1968, p. B1.

101. *New York Times,* August 16, 1968, p. 38.

102. *New York Times*, September 5, 1968, p. 1.

103. Chicago Study Team, p. xii.

104. Fogelson, pp. 224-225.

105. An example of this phenomenon seems to have been pointed to by the Commission's Chicago Study Team: "There has been no public condemnation of these violators of sound police procedures and common decency by either their commanding officers or city officials. Nor (at the time this Report is being completed — almost three months after the convention) has any disciplinary action been taken against most of them. That some policemen lost control of themselves under exceedingly provocative circumstances can perhaps be understood; but not condoned. If no action is taken against them, the effect can only be to discourage the majority of policemen who acted responsibly, and further weaken the bond between police and community." (p. xiii).

    Indeed, this might have been predicted from the lack of response to the Sparling Report on the police violence during the Chicago peace march of April 1968.

    According to a *Washington Post* study: "Criticism of the Chicago force has become a symbol of the 'lack of support' that policemen constantly bemoan. Policemen everywhere rallied to the defense of their Chicago colleagues. 'How can people defend the rights [sic] of that filth and attack good police officers?' asks Walter Fahey, a Boston patrolman." (*Washington Post*, December 15, 1968, p. B5). And a police chief is reported as observing that Chicago made police feel they had to defend rough and stupid police behavior because they felt criticism of Chicago police was criticism of police everywhere.

106. See John Hersey, *The Algiers Motel Incident* (New York: Bantam, 1968). Reportedly, ten black men and two white girls were severely beaten by police during the Detroit riots; three of the men were found dead, shot at close range, and the police involved failed to report the incident.

107. The following discussion is based on information which is readily available from sources such as the *New York Times* during the period discussed.

108. See, e.g., reports of Boston and Philadelphia in *San Francisco Chronicle*, December 16, 1968, p. 12.

109. An editor's note in a compendium of articles opposing review boards entitled "Police Review Boards," prepared by the National Fraternal Order of Police Committee on Human Rights and Law Enforcement, Cincinnati, Ohio, no date.

110. This discussion draws from the D. J. R. Bruckner article, *Los Angeles Times*, October 2, 1968, pp. 26 ff.

111. See also *New York Times*, November 3, 1968, p. 78; our interviews in Oakland, San Francisco, and New York; and Reichley for related information about the Wallace campaign of 1968.

112. *San Francisco Chronicle*, December 16, 1968, p. 12.

113. *Ibid.*
114. September 28, 1968, p. 9.
115. *Washington Post,* December 15, 1968, p. B1.
116. *Ibid.*
117. One of our staff was present at that reception.
118. *Washington Post,* December 15, 1968, p. B2.
119. *Ibid.*
120. *San Francisco Chronicle,* December 16, 1968, p. 12.
121. *Ibid.*
122. *San Francisco Chronicle,* December 18, 1968, p. 11.
123. John Harrington, National President of the Fraternal Order of Police, has launched a campaign urging Congress to reverse certain Supreme Court decisions on criminal justice, *San Francisco Chronicle,* December 16, p. 12.
124. *New York Times,* August 16, 1968, p. 38.
125. *New York Times,* September 3, 1968, p. 20; August 16, 1968, p. 38.
126. *New York Times,* August 16, 1968, p. 38.
127. *Ibid.*
128. *Washington Post,* December 15, 1968, p. B1.
129. Henry Wise, the labor lawyer retained to help organize and bargain for the Patrolmen's Association, as quoted in *Washington Post,* December 15, 1968, p. B2.
130. *Washington Post,* December 15, 1968, p. B1.
131. *Washington Post,* December 15, 1968, p. B2.
132. *Washington Post,* December 15, 1968, p. B1.
133. *Washington Post,* December 15, 1968, p. B2.
134. *Ibid.*
135. See 42 U.S.C. 1863.
136. For example, the National Defense Education Program, Chapter 17 of Title 20 of the U. S. Code, and the National Science Foundation, Chapter 16 of Title 42. Grants could also be made to existing institutions to establish special courses, much as the NDEP provides financial assistance to schools for teaching science, mathematics and foreign languages; and on-the-job summer training might also be provided. Such a program should be approached cautiously, however, in light of the current pressures to deny academic credit to Reserve Officer Training Corps and the comparatively low regard for policemen in the academic community.
137. See, e.g., "Task Force Report: The Police," *The President's Commission on Law Enforcement ...* , p. 142.
138. *Ibid..*
139. See Herbert L. Packer, *The Limits of the Criminal Sanction* (Palo Alto: Stanford University Press, 1968); The president's Commission on Law Enforcement and Administration of Justice, *The Challenge of Crime in a Free Society* (Washington, D. C.: U. S. Government Printing Office, February, 1967), p. 126; and Skolnick, "Coercion to Virtue," *Research*

Contribution of the American Bar Foundation, No. 7 (1968).
140. National Advisory Commission on Civil Disorder, pp. 311-312.